-직청직해의 바른길 빠른길-

시사영어청취의 실제

Practical Guides to the Current English Listening Skill

장경기 지음
서희숙 도움

UUP.

시사영어청취의 실제

Practical Guides to the Current English Listening Skills

2010년 8월 25일 1판 1쇄 인쇄
2010년 8월 31일 1판 1쇄 발행

지은이 | 장경기
발행인 | 김도연
발행처 | UUP(울산대학교출판부)

출판등록 | 제 370-1996-000001호(1996.3.13)
주소 | 680-749 울산광역시 남구 대학로 93 울산대학교 출판부
전화 | (052) 259-2488
팩스 | (052) 277-3011

값 12,000원

ISBN 978-89-7868-222-0 93740

* 잘못된 책은 바꿔드립니다.
* 울산대학교 출판부 홈페이지(http://uup.ulsan.ac.kr/)에서 무료 MP3파일을 다운로드 하실 수 있습니다.

●●● 머리말

心不在焉 視而不見 聽而不聞 食而不知其味 -大學-

(마음이 없으면 보아도 보이지 않고, 들어도 들리지 않으며, 먹어도 맛을 모르느니라.)

독해력(reading comprehension)의 이상적인 목표가 직독직해(直讀直解)에 있듯이 청해력(listening comprehension)의 이상적인 목표는 직청직해(直聽直解)에 있다. 직청직해는 화자의 말을 들으면서 동시에 이해하는 것이다. 이는 모국어에서는 무의식적으로 이루어지는 인지작용이다. 그러나 우리에게 영어는 모국어도 공용어도 아니고, 제2언어(second language)도 아닌 외국어(foreign language)이다. 외국어는 학습의 대상일 뿐 일상생활에서 사용되지 않으며, 이 점이 영어교육과 학습의 가장 큰 장애요인 중 하나이다.

우리의 이러한 외국어로서의 영어 교육환경에서 그동안 학습자의 독해력을 직독직해의 수준으로 끌어올리는 데는 어느 정도 성공하였다. 이는 말할 것도 없이 읽기는 문자 매체를 대상으로 하기 때문이다. 필자는 우리나라의 듣기교육도 직청직해가 가능한 시대에 접어들었다고 감히 판단하였다. 그 근거는 두 가지다. 첫째, Internet의 덕분으로 영어 모국어화자의 원음 자료를 아주 쉽게 접할 수 있고, 저장도 가능하여 이제 소리의 시간성을 뛰어넘어 문자매체의 장점인 공간화가 가능해졌기 때문이다. 둘째, 기존의 청취력 교육 및 학습 방법의 치명적인 허점을 극복하는 것이 충분히 가능하다는 것을 학문적으로나 경험적으로 확신하였기 때문이다. 한마디로 기존 청취력 교육은 영어의 물리적 소리(physical sound)에 익숙해지도록 하는 교육이었다고 해도 과언이 아니다. 바꿔 말하면 그것은 거의 대부분 청력(hearing ability) 교육이었지 청취력(listening capability), 즉 청취 이해력(listening comprehension)의 진정한 영어교육이 아니었다고 감히 말할 수 있다. 이제 물리적 청력 교육에서 심리적 청취력 교육으로 전환해야 하고, 또 그렇게 할 수 있는 여건이 마련된 시점임을 확신한다.

필자는 이제 직청직해를 위한 진정한 청해력 교육을 제안하며, 이의 구체적인 실천 방안을 이 교재에서 두 가지 관점에서 제시하기로 하겠다.

첫째, 청취력 교육과 학습은 통합적 접근법(integrated approach)으로 이루어져야 한다. 다시 말하면 듣기능력이 다른 언어능력과 완전히 독립된 능력이 아니므로 그 교육과 학습도 모든 영역의 언어능력을 동원하여 더 나은 종합적인 능력으로 향상시키는 과정의 하나로 이루어져야 한다. 이는 듣는 과정도 청취력만을 발휘해서 듣는 것이 아니고 종합적인 언어능력과 비언어적 인지능력을 총동원하여 소리매체를 해석한다는 것을 의미한다. 언어능력은 문법(grammar)이며, 그 안에는 소리의 문법, 어휘의 문법, 문장의 문법, 의미론, 화용론이 모두 다 포함된다. 비언어적 지식도 매우 중요하다. 한마디로 비언어적 지식은 백과사전적 지식이다. 화자와 청자는 물론 문장이 사용되는 환경에 관한 모든 지식이다. 화자와 청자는 이 지식을 총동원하여 언어를 표현하고, 동시에 해석한다. 청취력의 교육과 학습 과정에서도 이 비언어적 지식을 모두 발휘하도록 도모해야 한다.

둘째, 청취력의 교육 및 학습 자료는 지속적으로 접근가능한 최대한의 진정성을 담보하는 것이어야 한다. 그것은 학습자의 지적 수준에 맞고, 흥미와 관심을 끌 수 있는 정보를 담고 있으며, 교양있는 세계인이 사용하는 품위있는 영어이어야 한다. 이 조건에 합치되는 자료는 바로 세계적인 방송 미디어의 시사영어(current English)라고 우리는 판단하였다. 시사영어는 매일 우리와 호흡을 같이 하는 사건, 사고 및 여러 분야의 유익하고 생생한 정보를 담고 있는 동시대의 살아있는 영어로서, 끊임없이 전세계의 안방으로 전달되고 있다.

직청직해의 청해력을 신장하기 위해서는 듣고자 하는 정보에 대한 학습자의 욕구 및 학습 동기는 학습자가 언어적, 비언어적 지식을 총동원하여 집중적으로 듣도록 유인하는 결정적인 추진력이 된다. 물에 빠진 사람이 살기 위하여 지푸라기라도 잡는 심정을 (A drowning man will catch at a straw.) 상상할 수 있다면 그 학습자는 직청직해에 도달할 수 있는 인지적 자격이 있다고 감히 말할 수 있다. 더구나 이런 살아있는 뉴스를 저장해서 무한히 반복해서 들을 수 있고, 동시에 텍스트로 전환하여 읽을 수 있는 시대에 살고 있는 우리로서는 바야흐로 직청직해를 성취할 수 있는 가장 좋은 여건을 갖추고 있으며, 이제 이를 어떻게, 얼마나 효과적으로 활용하느냐 하는 과제만 남은 셈이다. 이는 한마디로 말하면 귀의 작업(ear work)을 최대화하고, 눈의 작업(eye work)은 최소화하는 것이다. 또한 귀의 작업은 말은 곧 마음의 작업(mind work)을 의미하는 것임은 두말할 필요가 없을 것이다. 우리가 매 단원을 '마음으로 듣기'로 시작하게 되는데, 이는 곧 소리를 의미와 연결시키기 위하여 온 마음을 다 쏟아 부으라는 것이다. (Oh, Mindful Learning!)

필자가 이상과 같은 결론에 도달하고 학생들에게 교육을 해온지가 2003년이니까 어느덧 8년째이다. 필자가 교환교수로 미국에 다녀온 다음 해였다. 여러 가지 경험을 쌓고, 깨달은 점도 많았지만 "미국교민이 30년을 넘게 그곳에 살면서도 매일매일 CNN도, NBC도 제대로 듣지 못한다는 엄연한 사실"이 그동안 영어에 대한 학문적 접근에 안주한 필자에게 충격적인 것이었다. 그곳 대학에서 청강을 하면서도 교수의 말은 그런대로 알아듣겠는데, 학생들의 질문과 교수의 답변은 갑자기 빨라져서 거의 깜깜하였다. 부끄럽기도 하고, 분하기도 하였다. 하지만 가끔씩 거주하는 동네를 산책하다가 나에게 길을 묻는 운전자들에게 큰소리로 복수하여 스트레스를 풀기도 하였다. "그렇다. 문제는 청취력이다!" 귀국후 마음의 짐을 풀기 위하여 Internet site를 둘러보다가 운 좋게 <ganaro.com>을 만났고, 학교에서 마침 새로운 강의개설의 여건도 주어져서 처음에 TDC 강의로 시작했으며, 곧 계절학기로 확대, 발전하였다. 그동안 많은 수강생과 함께 즐거운 시간을 가졌으나, 한 두 가지 아쉬운 점은 교재가 정해져있지 않아서 예습과 복습을 하기가 불편하다는 점과 빈칸을 듣고 메우기가 좀 더 단계적으로 구성되어서 수준별 학습이 이루어졌으면 하는 점이었다. 학습효과라는 면에서 이 두 가지는 매우 중요한데, 이를 해결하기 위해서는 교재의 편찬이 필수적이라고 판단하였고 이제 결실을 맺게 된 것이다.

끝으로 몇 분께 고마운 인사로 마무리하기로 하겠다. 먼저 <ganaro.com>을 설립하여 수익성이 거의 없이 운영하면서 우리나라 영어청취교육에 일조한 이건일님께 감사드린다. 다행히 필자와 이메일로 연락이 되어 그동안의 자료를 자유롭게 사용하도록 흔쾌히 허락해주셨다. 이제 서희숙 선생께 깊은 감사를 드린다. 서선생은 학부와 대학원에서 필자와 사제지가연을 맺은 재원으로 실제로 필자의 청취강의를 들은 바도 있으며, 나의 출판 의지에 공감하고 번거로운 Word 작업 이상의 일들을 기꺼이 맡아주었다. 마지막으로 출판을 허락해준 출판부장 박삼수 교수님과 복더위에 수고해준 편집진 자매님들께 깊이 감사드린다.

2010년 8월
문수골 인문학당에서
장경기

○ 교재의 구성

이 청취 교재는 총 3부로 구성되어 있으며, 대학에서 학기 단위로 교육할 수 있도록 제1부와 제2부는 15장의 독립된 주제로 구성되어 있고, 제3부는 제1부와 제2부의 텍스트를 다시 종합하여 새롭게 빈칸을 만들어서 듣고 채우도록 문제화하였고, 새로 추가한 자료로 듣기 문제화한 15장 등 모두 45장의 독립적인 단원으로 구성되어 있다.

또한 제1부와 제2부의 난이도에는 큰 차이가 없으며, 각 장은 동일한 내용의 시사관련 텍스트를 아래와 같이 5단계로 나누어 반복적으로 청취 연습하는 과정에서 문장의 구조와 의미를 직접 연결시키는 직청직해의 최종적인 목표에 도달하도록 구성되어 있다. 아울러 각 단원 마다 꼭 필요한 경우에 텍스트의 내용 및 구조와 관련된 부분에 대한 해설과 발음 및 구조에 관한 간단한 설명을 추가하였으니 가볍게 읽어주기 바란다.

[1] 마음으로 듣기

텍스트를 보지 않고 오디오를 듣는 과정으로서, 청취력 연습의 1단계이다. 눈을 감거나 편안한 자세로, 가벼운 마음으로 들어본다. 각 단원의 제목이 내용을 파악하는 중요한 단서가 되며, 전체의 내용을 대충이나마 파악해 본다.

[2] (중심어구) 듣기

각 단원의 텍스트를 제시하고 그 안에서 내용의 특성에 따라 가장 두드러진 단어나 구를 빈칸으로 만들어 오디오를 듣고 채워나가는 청취력 연습의 단계이다. 학습자는 텍스트의 보이는 부분의 도움을 받아서 전체의 내용을 이해하는 것을 목표로 삼으며, 보이지 않는 어구를 문장의 내용과 일치하도록 채우게 된다.

[3] 확장형

중심어구 듣기가 주로 어휘범주, 즉 품사 중심이며, 확장형은 머리어를 확장한 형태인 구범주를 듣고 채우는 청취력 연습의 단계이다. 문장을 올바로 이해하기 위해서는 단어가 구가 되는 문법을 아는 것이 필수적이다. 이 확장형 연습을 통해서 구조를 더 잘 이해할 수 있게 된다.

[4] 연결음 듣기

이 단계에서는 각각의 고유한 음이 다른 음과 연결되어 일어나는 변화를 집중해서 연습하게 된다. 특히 음절과 음절, 단어와 단어 사이에서 여러 유형의 동화현상이 발생하는데, 이 점에 유의하여 빈 칸에 채워 넣는 과정이다.

[5] 응용형

앞 단계까지의 종합단계이자 추가적으로 연습할 필요가 있는 항목을 빈칸으로 남겨서 최종적으로 정리하고 확인하는 과정이다.

○ 교재의 효과적인 사용법

(1) 교재를 구입한 학생은 울산대학교 출판부 homepage의 게시판/자료실에 들어가서 필요한 오디오 파일을 내려받아 사용할 수 있다. 해당 오디오 파일명은 각 단원 제목 옆에 (   ) 안에 표기하였다. 출판부 homepage: //uup.ulsan.ac.kr

<예시> 1.1 This Is Today In History (0201gandhi)

<오디오파일명>

(2) 학습자는 각 단원의 지시에 따라 학습하며, 다른 단원을 참고로 하여 미리 빈칸의 정답을 알고 들으면 학습효과가 반감되므로 스스로 이 원칙을 준수해야 한다.

(3) 학습자는 스스로 정답을 찾아낼 때까지 반복해서 들으면서 그 과정에서 자신에게 필요한 혹은 부족한 지식이 무엇인지 알아내고, 이를 보충하도록 노력해야 한다. 발음, 단어, 구조에 관한 지식, 그리고 모든 상식과 추론능력 등을 동원하여 마치 무인도에서 암호문을 해독하지 않으면 살아나갈 수 없다는 심정으로 의미를 구조와 연결시키는 법칙을 즉시화, 자동화해야 한다. 학문에 왕도는 없다. (There is no royal road to learning!) 그러나 뜻이 있는 곳에 길이 있고 (Where there is a will, there is a way.), 그 길은 자신이 찾아야 한다. 나는 나야!

텍스트를 들으면서 효율성을 높이기 위해서 할 수 있는 구체적인 방법은 다음과 같다. 자신에게 맞는 더 나은 방법이면 더 좋을 것이다.

① 오디오를 들으면서 끊어지는 곳은 사선(slash)으로 표시해둔다

<예시> I sent a letter / to my mother / two weeks ago.

② 강세가 낯선 단어가 나오면 즉시 그 단어의 모음 위에 강세표시(')를 해둔다.

<예시> addítion, conféssion

③ 발음이 연결되면 이음줄(slur)로 표시해둔다.

<예시> in⁀the room

④ 문장 안에서 단일한 구조임을 표시하려면 중괄호로 표시해둔다.

<예시> [Something unexpected] has happened

⑤ 빈칸을 채울 때는 볼펜으로 적어두어서 정답에 이르는 과정을 다시 복습하는 자료로 활용한다.

⑥ 필요하면 메모(note-taking)를 적극적으로 활용한다.

⑦ 오디오를 들으면서 자동적으로 따라서 말해보는(follow-repeating) 것을 습관화한다. 이는 일종의 흉내바둑 같은 것으로 혀를 훈련하고 리듬감을 익힐 수 있다.

⑧ 무엇보다도 영어의 종합적인 능력을 주도적으로 기르는 자료로 활용하는 자세가 필요하다.

(4) 학습자는 필요하면 오디오의 속도를 달리 하면서 마치 자동차 운전을 연습하듯이 속도감, 즉 리듬을 익혀가는 것이 중요하다. 정상속도로 들리지 않는 부분이 느린 속도에서 들릴 경우도 있고, 빠른 속도에 어느 정도 익숙해지면 정상속도도 낯설지 않게 되어 자신이 생기게 된다.

(5) 주어진 텍스트의 내용을 다 완전히 이해할 때쯤에는 듣기만으로도 내용을 알 수 있게 되므로, 마침내 직청직해의 목표에 도달하게 된 것이다. 그러나 여기에서 중단하지 말고 텍스트 없이 이미 배운 내용을 자주 들으면서 즐겁게 정진해나간다면 어느덧 자신이 영어에 자유로운 경지에 들어서 있음을 실감하게 되리라 확신한다.

●●● 목차

✓Part 3

1 실전편

2 실전편

3 실전 완결편

Part 1

01.

0201gandhi

This Is Today In History

1 마음으로 듣기

▸ This is [Today In History].
이 표현은 "이 시간은 '역사속의 오늘' 혹은 '오늘의 역사시간'입니다"라는 프로그램을 소개하는 일반화된 방송용 어구이다.

▸ The Associated Press: AP(연합)통신사

2 한정사 듣기

This is Today In History.

Making headlines on _________ day in 1948, many across India and the world were stunned to hear of _________ assassination of 78-year-old Mahatma Gandhi, _______ _______________ spiritual leader.

_______ British-educated lawyer was gunned down while walking to _____ evening prayer meeting.

A young man stepped from _________ crowd of about 500 and shot Gandhi in ______ chest and abdomen.

Riots quickly swept Bombay when news of _____ ____________ death was received.

The Associated Press reported that 15 persons were killed and more than fifty injured in _______ riots.

▸ 한정사(determiner)는?

① 명사구(noun phrase)의 맨 앞에 오는 지정어(specifier)이다.

② 머리어(head)인 명사의 구체적인 자질을 지정해주는 기능범주이며, 머리어와 수의 일치를 이룬다.

e.g. a good boy / two good boys, this book / these books

③ 한정사는 관사(a/the), 지시형용사(this, that, these, those), 수나 양을 표현하는 양화사 each, every, any, some, all, several, many, much, more), 소유형용사(my, your, his, her, its, our, their) 및 모든 명사구(NP)의 소유격 표현 등이 있다.

3 확장형

This is Today In History.

Making headlines _______ ________ ______ in 1948, many across India and were stunned to hear of the assassination of 78-year-old Mahatma Gandhi, __________ ___________ _____________ leader.

The British-educated lawyer was gunned down while walking to an evening prayer meeting.

A young men stepped from ______ _________ of about 500 and shot Gandhi in _______ _________ and abdomen.

Riots quickly swept Bombay when news of ______ ___________ _________ was received.

The Associated Press reported that 15 persons were killed and more than fifty injured _____ _______ ________.

▸ 청취력은 예측력/추리력/눈치력이 절반?

여러분이 미국인 친구에게 이렇게 물었다고 하자. "How old is your father?" 친구의 대답은 기대와 달리 아주 짧게, 그것도 빠르게 나왔다. "Fiftee-." 평소에도 숫자를 영어로 알아듣는데 어려움이 있던 터라 바로 머리에 들어오지 않았다. "15 세야, 50 세야?" 이때 여러분의 머리는 번개처럼 움직인다. 그 결과 저 친구가 한말은 "Fifteen."이 아니고 "Fifty." 임이 분명하다고 결론을 내린다. (그 이유는 여러분이 더 잘 안다!) 이러한 무의식적인 인지능력은 청취력에서도 엄청난 위력을 발휘한다. 더 정확히 말하면 이 능력을 최대한도로 활용하느냐가 여러분의 청취력을 결정한다고 해도 과언이 아니다. 여러분이 지금부터 직접 체험해보시길 바란다.

4 연결음 듣기

This is Today In History.

Making headlines on this day in 1948, many across India and the world were ________________ _____ hear of the assassination of 78-year-old Mahatma Gandhi, the ______________ ________________ leader.

The British-educated lawyer was ___________ ________ while walking to an evening prayer meeting.

A young man _____________ _________ the crowd of about 500 and shot Gandhi in the chest _______ ______________.

Riots quickly swept Bombay when ________ _____ Mr. Gandhi's death was received.

The Associated Press reported that 15 persons were __________ ______ more than fifty injured in the riots.

▸ 영어의 자음(consonant)은?

① 유성음과 무성음으로 나누어진다.

② 모음(vowel)의 앞과 뒤에 놓여 음절을 구성하며, 자음이 연속 나오기도 한다.

e.g. strike, West Bank

③ 단어의 끝에 오면 귀에 들리지 않을 정도로 약하게 발음되지만(unreleased), 그 뒤에 모음이 오면 다시 음이 살아나서 그 모음과 연결될 수도 있다.

5 응용형

This is Today In History.

Making _________________ on this day in 1948, many across India and the world were stunned to hear of the assassination of 78-year-old Mahatma Gandhi, the country's spiritual ____________.

The British-educated ____________ was gunned down while walking to an evening prayer meeting.

A young man stepped from the __________ of about 500 and ________ Gandhi in the chest and abdomen.

Riots quickly __________ Bombay when news of Mr. Gandhi's death was received.

The Associated Press ______________ that 15 persons were killed and more than fifty injured in the ________.

02.

0202muslim

A Muslim Cleric Released In Israel

1 마음으로 듣기

▸ Imam: (회교국의) 종교적 원수의 칭호 (=Imaum)

▸ rather than face new terror charges
(새로운 테러 혐의를 당하기보다는 차라리 ...)
'rather than' 다음에 원형동사구문 ('to' 없는 동사구문)이 오는 중요한 구문이다.

2 전치사 듣기

______ Israel, a military judge has ordered the release _____ a prominent Muslim leader deported _________ the United States.

Fawaz Damra is the former Imam _____ Ohio's largest mosque.

He was arrested in 2004 on charge __________ concealing ties ___________ the Palestinian group Islamic Jihad.

He agreed _____ deportation last year rather than face new terror charges.

Israeli authorities immediately detained Damra _________ his deportation _____ the West Bank earlier this month.

_____ ordering Damra's release, the Israeli military judge said there is insufficient evidence _____ hold him any longer.

▸ 전치사(preposition)는?

① 전치사구(preposition phrase; PP)의 머리어(head)이다.
② 전치사는 자신의 목적어에게 목적격을 부여한다.
③ 전치사의 목적어는 일반적으로 명사구(noun phrase)이다. 동사구가 전치사의 목적어로 쓰이려면 동명사형(gerund), 즉 -ing 구조를 갖는다.

3 확장형

_____ ___________, a military judge has ordered ______ _________ _____ a prominent Muslim leader deported from the United States.

Fawaz Damra is the former Imam at Ohio's largest mosque.

He was arrested in 2004 _______ ___________ _______ concealing ties to the Palestinian group Islamic Jihad.

He __________ _____ deportation last year rather than face new terror charges.

Israeli authorities immediately detained Damra __________ _______ _________ to the West Bank earlier this month.

_____ _______________ Damra's release, the Israeli military judge said there is insufficient evidence to hold him any longer.

4 연결음 듣기

In Israel, a military has ________ ______ release of a prominent Muslim leader deported from the United States.

Fawaz Damra is the former Imam _____ _________ largest mosque.

He was arrested in 2004 on __________ _____ concealing ties to the Palestinian group Islamic Jihad.

He agreed to deportation _______ _______ rather than face new terror charges.

Israeli authorities immediately ______________ ________ after his deportation to the West Bank earlier this month.

In ordering Damra's release, the Israeli military judge ___________ ___________ ___________ insufficient evidence to hold him any longer.

▸ 영어의 모음은?

① 음절의 핵(nucleus)이다. 따라서 모음의 수는 음절의 수와 같다.

② 강세(stress)가 주어진다.

③ 단어의 경계를 넘어서 앞뒤 자음과 연결음이 될 수 있다.

5 응용형

In Israel, a military judge has ordered the release of a prominent Muslim leader ____________________ from the United States.

Fawaz Damra is the former Imam at Ohio's largest mosque.

He was _______________ in 2004 on charge of ___________________ ties to the Palestinian group Islamic Jihad.

He agreed to ___________________ last year rather than face new terror charges.

Israeli authorities _____________________ detained Damra after his deportation to the West Bank earlier this month.

In ordering Damra's release, the Israeli military judge said there is ________________ evidence to hold him any longer.

03.

0203beach

The Beach Open To Everyone

1 마음으로 듣기

▸ No maids [are] allowed.
문법적으로는 수동문의 조동사 'are'가 필요하지만, 신문의 headline처럼 보도의 시작에서 생략된 것이다.

▸ human rights: 인권(복수형에 유의)

2 한정사 듣기

No maids allowed. It's _______ law.

_______ law at _________ luxury beach resort in Peru prohibits domestic workers from getting in the water with __________ employers.

800 employees of _____ rich protested against _____ law at a beach, South of Lima.

At first they formed ______ human chain to block access and then they illegally jumped into _______ Ocean.

According to human rights organizations, _______ beach resort, known as Asia, is _________ place where social and racial discrimination are commonplace.

Beyond being prohibited from swimming in ______ Ocean, domestic employees have reported being excluded from restaurants and from just being on _______ Beach.

Peruvian laws state that _______ beach is open to _______ citizens.

▸ 명사구는?

① 한정사를 지정어로 하는 문장을 구성하는 핵심적인 구범주이다.

② 문장 안에서의 명사구의 대표적인 기능은 주어(subject), 목적어(object), 전치사의 목적어, 보어 등이다.

③ 한정사는 명사구를 인식하는 중요한 표지이며, 명사구는 문장의 주어나 목적어 등의 중요한 기능을 담당한다.

3 확장형

No maids allowed. It's the law.

The law at _____ __________ beach resort in Peru prohibits domestic workers from getting in the water with ________ __________________.

800 employees of ___________ _____________ protested against _____________ ___________ at a beach, South of Lima.

At first they formed _____ __________ chain to block access and then they illegally jumped into the Ocean.

According to human rights organizations, _________ __________ resort, known as Asia, is _____ _________ where social and racial discrimination are commonplace.

Beyond being prohibited from swimming in ______ _________, domestic employees have reported being excluded from restaurants and from just being on _________ __________.

Peruvian laws state that the beach is open to _______ ________________.

4 연결음 듣기

No maids allowed. It's the law.

The law at this luxury beach resort in Peru prohibits domestic workers from getting in the water ________ __________ employers.

800 employees of the rich protested ____________ _______ law at a beach, South of Lima.

At first they __________ _____ human chain to block access and then they illegally jumped into the Ocean.

According to human rights organizations, this beach resort, known as Asia, __________ _____ place where social and racial discrimination are commonplace.

Beyond being prohibited from swimming in the Ocean, domestic employees have reported being excluded from restaurants and from ________ __________ on the Beach.

Peruvian laws __________ _______ the beach is open to all citizens.

▸ 발음(pronunciation/sound)과 철자(spelling/letter)의 관계는?

① 발음은 선사시대부터, 철자는 유사시대 이후에 생겼다.

② 발음은 시간언어, 철자는 공간언어이다.

③ 발음과 철자는 일치할 수 없고, 발음기호조차도 실제 발음과 같을 수 없다.

5 응용형

No __________ allowed. It's the law.

The law at this luxury beach resort in Peru ______________ domestic workers from getting in the water with their employers.

800 employees of the rich ________________ against that law at a beach, South of Lima.

At first they formed a human chain to _________ _________ and then they illegally jumped into the Ocean.

According to human rights organizations, this beach resort, known as Asia, is a place where social and racial ________________________ are commonplace.

Beyond being _______________ from swimming in the Ocean, domestic employees have reported being ______________ from restaurants and from just being on the Beach.

Peruvian _________ state that the beach is open to all citizens.

04. Smoking Bans Are Popular

0127smoking

1 마음으로 듣기

▸ "obesity paradox"
과체중이 심장병의 위험을 줄인다는 역설은 금연함으로써 (일시적으로) 체중이 늘어나는 점과 관련되어 있다.

2 -ing형 동사 듣기

For the first time in the nation's history, more than half of Americans live in a city or state that bans __________ in workplaces, restaurants, or bars.

The movement for smoke-free air began in Berkley, Calif., 30 years ago.

__________ bans have also become more popular globally, with laws in place in countries __________ Ireland, Italy and Spain.

And ________ overweight may reduce the risk of ________ from heart failure.

New research indicates that obese patients hospitalized with heart failure tend to fare better than their lean counterparts.

The report, which appears in the American Heart Journal, showed that the "obesity paradox" may also apply to patients with rapidly _____________ or "decompensated" heart failure.

▸ [smoking bans]
'smoking bans'는 복합명사구(compound)로서 명사 'smoking'은 뒤에 오는 머리어 명사 'bans'의 수식어로 쓰였고 '금연'의 의미가 된다.

▸ [... bans smoking ...]
[... bans [smoking in workplaces]...]은 동사구로서 'smoking'은 타동사 'ban'의 목적어로 쓰인 동사구 'smoke in workplaces'의 동명사형이다. 의미는 "(작업장에서) 담배피우는 것을 금지하 ..."가 된다.

3 확장형

For the first time in the nation's history, more than half of Americans live in a city or state that bans ________ _____ ____________, restaurants, or bars.

The movement for smoke-free air began in Berkley, Calif., 30 years ago.

_________ _______ have also become more popular globally, with laws in place in countries _________ ________, Italy, and Spain.

And ________ ___________ may reduce the risk _____ ________ from heart failure.

New research indicates that obese patients hospitalized with heart failure tend to fare better than their lean counterparts.

The report, which appears in the American Heart Journal, showed that the "obesity paradox" may also apply to patients ______ rapidly __________ or "decompensated" heart failure.

▸ 일반적으로 한국인에게 어려운 발음은?

① 우리말에 없거나 구별이 어려운 자음: [θ, ð, f, v]

e.g. sink/think, dough/though, base/vase, pace/face, of/off

② 조음위치가 애매한 모음: [i, e, æ]

e.g. sit, set, sat

③ 순자음도 순모음도 아닌 음: [l, r, w, j]

e.g. lice/rice, long/wrong, word/world, year/ear

그러나 더욱 중요한 사실은 이 단어들도 문장 안에서 쓰이면 우리의 또다른 인식능력인 예측력에 의해서 올바른 단어를 찾아간다는 점이다.

4 연결음 듣기

For the _______ _______ in the nation's history, more than half of Americans live in a city or state that bans smoking in workplaces, _____________, _____ bars.

The movement for smoke-free air began in Berkley, Calif., 30 years ago.

Smoking ___________ _____________ also become more popular globally, with ___________ ___________ place in countries including Ireland, Italy, and Spain.

And being overweight may reduce the risk of dying from _________ __________.

New research indicates that obese patients hospitalized with heart failure ______ _______ fare better than their lean counterparts.

The report, ________ ___________ in the American Heart Journal, showed that the "obesity paradox" may also __________ _______ patients with rapidly worsening or "decompensated" heart failure.

▸ 가장 짧은 단어는?

① 하나의 모음으로 만들어진 'a'이다.

② 자음(C)과 모음(V)이 교차하여 만들어진 단어가 가장 자연스러우나, 대부분의 단어는 이러한 배열을 가지고 있지 않다.

(C)(C)(C)V(C)(C)(C)

e.g. strike, scream, splash / prompt, distinct, glimpse, jinx, text, midst

③ 단어의 경계를 넘어서면 연결음은 더욱 길어지고 복잡해진다.

e.g. ice cream / I scream. / iced tea

5 응용형

For the first time in the nation's history, more than _______ of Americans live in a city or state that _________ smoking in workplaces, restaurants, or bars.

The movement for smoke-free air began in Berkley, Calif., 30 years ago.

Smoking bans have also __________ more popular globally, _______ laws in place in countries including Ireland, Italy, and Spain.

And being overweight may ___________ the risk of dying from heart failure.

New research indicates that obese patients hospitalized with heart failure tend to ___________ better than their lean counterparts.

The report, which appears in the American Heart Journal, _________ that the "obesity paradox" may also apply to patients with rapidly _____________ or "decompensated" heart failure.

...05.

0203vista

New Operating System Vista

1 마음으로 듣기

▸ the-gotta-have-it-now message

You've got to (=gotta) have it now. (지금 안사면 후회할 거야.)

위 표현의 일부를 hyphen(-)으로 연결하여 복합어를 만들었다.

2 인칭대명사 'it' 듣기

Microsoft has introduced what ______ says is the next big thing in software.

Microsoft calls ______ the biggest software launch ever.

Five million people signed up to test ________ new operating system called Vista, and in _________ splashy party in a Times Square theater, Chairman Bill Gates promised _____________ would integrate the functions of the computer from entertainment to editing better than ever.

"Homes are expecting now to have integration, to be able to get their photos up in their living room, to be able to organize things."

Despite the gotta-have- _____ -now message of the launch, CEO Steve Ballmer concedes most users will wait till their next computer to get Vista.

Though, the company insists the look of ______ alone will dazzle the customers.

▸ 인칭대명사 'it'는?

① 중성, 단수 인칭대명사로서 주어, 목적어, 소유격 한정사(its)로 쓰인다.

② 반드시 선행하는 단수명사구를 대신한다.

③ 날씨의 'it'나 허사의 'it'와 엄격히 구분된다.

3 확장형

Microsoft has introduced what ______ ________ is the next big thing in software.

Microsoft _________ _______ the biggest software launch ever.

Five million people signed up to test ______ ______ operating system called Vista, and in _____ ____________ party in a Times Square theater, Chairman Bill Gates promised it would integrate the functions of the computer from entertainment to editing better than ever.

"Homes are expecting now to have integration, to be able to get their photos up in their living room, to be able to organize things."

Despite the gotta-_________-______-______ message of the launch, CEO Steve Ballmer concedes most users will wait till their next computer to get Vista.

Though, the company insists the look of ____ _________ will dazzle the customers.

▸ Microsoft has introduced [what it says [t] is the next big thing in software].

① what~이하 절은 주절 어휘동사 'introduced'의 목적절이다.

② 'what'은 선행사를 포함한 관계사이다.

③ 'what'은 'says' 다음의 [t] 자리에서 'is'의 주어 역할을 하며, 이때 what~이하 절은 선행하는 어휘동사 'says'의 목적절이다. (t = trace = 이동전의 자리)

④ 'what'은 [t] 자리에서 다시 'it says' 앞자리로 이동한다.

이러한 구조를 Pushdown Construction이라 부르기도 하는데, 일종의 이중 내포구조(double embedded construction)이고, 매우 자주 쓰이는 구문이다.

4 연결음 듣기

Microsoft has introduced what it _________ _____ the next big thing in software.

Microsoft calls it the biggest software launch ever.

Five million people signed up to test its new operating system called Vista, _________ _____ its splashy party in a Times Square theater, Chairman Bill Gates promised it would integrate the _______________ _____ the computer from entertainment to editing better than ever.

"________ ______ expecting now to have integration, to be able to get their _____________ ______ in their living room, to be able to organize things."

Despite the gotta-have-it-now ____________ _____ the launch, CEO Steve Ballmer concedes _________ ___________ will wait till their next computer to get Vista.

Though, the company insists the ________ _____ it alone will dazzle the customers.

▸ 가장 긴 영어 단어는?

① SmileS

시작과 끝이 'mile'이나 되니까! (Humor!)

② 이론적으로 가장 긴 단어도 없고, 가장 긴 문장도 없다.

③ 이유는 아무리 길어도 거기에다 다시 더 긴 단어나 문장을 만들 수 있기 때문이다. 같은 이유로 단어의 수나 문장의 수도 그 생성규칙에 따라 무한정 늘어날 수 있다.

5 응용형

Microsoft has ______________ what it says is the next big thing in software.

Microsoft calls it the biggest software ___________ ever.

Five million people _________ up to test its new operating system called _______, and in its splashy party in a Times Square theater, Chairman Bill Gates promised it would __________ the functions of the computer from entertainment to editing better than ever.

"Homes are expecting now to have _____________, to be able to get their photos up in their living room, to be able to organize things."

___________ the gotta-have-it-now message of the launch, CEO Steve Ballmer __________________ most users will wait till their next computer to get Vista.

Though, the company insists the look of it alone will ___________ the customers.

▸ 직청직해의 단서는?

① 시간적 순서(Expressions of Time Order)

First, Second, Then, Last, Finally, Before, After

② 관점의 이동(Transitional Markers)

Therefore, And, Then, However, On the contrary, Otherwise, Though

③ 예시(Showing examples)

For example, For instance, Take for instance, Let's say, In our example

④ 화제의 변경(Change of Topics)

As for, Speaking of, By the way, In addition (to)

06. Pharmaceutical Giant Novartis

0205pharma

1 마음으로 듣기

▸ Novartis: 미국의 거대 제약회사로서 다국적기업이다.

2 조동사(시제동사 포함) 듣기

Protests ________ held in Washington and New Delhi, India on Monday against the pharmaceutical giant Novartis.

The company ______ seeking to overturn an Indian law regarding drug patents.

Demonstrators _______ that if Norvatis ________ the lawsuit, it ________ threaten India's stability to manufacture low cost generic drugs that _______ distributed throughout the global South to treat AIDS and other diseases.

Monique Wanjala __________ in New Delhi.

"I ________ ________ living with HIV for the last."

"This is thirteen years now, and I _________ ________ on treatment on ARVs since 2004, and this is because access ________ __________ made easier, and we ________ saying that if Novartis go through with this case, what ______ it mean to us as people living with HIV? It _________ that our lives are at stake."

In Washington, activists from the Global AIDS Alliance ________ to deliver a mini coffin to the downtown office of Novartis.

▸ 조동사(auxiliary)는?

① 본동사를 도와주는 보조동사(helping verb)이다.

② 한 시제절에 조동사가 없을 수도 있고, 최대 4개까지 나올 수 있다.

Tense (Modal) (Aspect(perfect/progressive)) (Passive) + V ...

③ 시제절 안에서 맨 앞에 나오는 조동사에 시제(tense)가 표시된다. 이 조동사를 운용자(operator)라 부른다.

3 확장형

Protests _______ ________ in Washington and New Delhi, India on Monday against the pharmaceutical giant Novartis.

The company _____ ___________ to overturn an Indian law regarding drug patents.

Demonstrators ________ ________ if Norvatis wins the lawsuit, it ______ _________ India's stability to manufacture low cost generic drugs that _______ _______________ throughout the global South to treat AIDS and other diseases.

Monique Wanjala spoke in New Delhi.

"I ________ ________ ________ with HIV for the last."

"This is thirteen years now, and I have been on treatment on ARVs since 2004, and this is because access _________ ___________ ________ easier, and we _______ _________ that if Novartis go through with this case, what ________ it _______ to us as people living with HIV? It ___________ ________ our lives are at stake."

In Washington, activists from the Global AIDS Alliance _________ ________ deliver a mini coffin to the downtown office of Novartis.

4 연결음 듣기

Protests were _______ _____ Washington and New Delhi, India on Monday against the pharmaceutical giant Novartis.

The company is seeking to _________ ______ Indian law regarding drug patents.

Demonstrators say _______ _____ Norvatis wins the lawsuit, it will threaten India's stability to manufacture low cost generic drugs _________ _________ distributed throughout the global South to treat AIDS ______ _______ diseases.

Monique Wanjala _______ _____ New Delhi.

"I ______ ______ living with HIV for the last."

"This is thirteen years now, and I _____ ______ on treatment on ARVs since 2004, and this is because access has been made easier, and we are saying ___________ _______ Novartis go through with this case, what does it mean to us as people living with HIV? It means ________ _______ _________ are at stake."

In Washington, activists from the Global AIDS Alliance try to deliver a mini coffin to the downtown _________ _____ Novartis.

▸ 가장 잘 들리는 영어 단어는?

① 자신의 영어 이름이다.

자신이 가장 잘 알고 다른 단어와 구분되는 고유명사이기 때문이다. 반면에 처음 듣는 다른 사람의 이름이나 지명 등의 고유명사는 알아듣기가 어렵다.

② 고유명사는 어떤 한정사나 수식어가 붙지 않는다. 역설적으로 알아듣기 어려운 단어가 어떤 한정사나 수식어도 붙지 않았다면 고유명사로 해석할 수 있고, 그것이 고유명사의 의미의 전부이다.

③ 물론 자신이 아는 단어는 더 잘 들린다. 그러나 문맥과 일치하는 의미인지를 확인 하는데는 더 차원 높은 복잡한 지식이 필요하다.

5 응용형

____________ were held in Washington and New Delhi, India on Monday ________ the pharmaceutical giant Novartis.

The company is seeking to ________ an Indian law regarding drug patents.

Demonstrators say that if Norvatis wins the __________, it will threaten India's ________________ to manufacture low cost generic drugs that are distributed ______________ the global South to treat AIDS and other diseases.

Monique Wanjala spoke in New Delhi.

"I have been living with HIV for the last."

"This is thirteen years now, and I have been on ________ on ARVs since 2004, and this is _________ access has been made easier, and we are saying that if Novartis go through with this case, _______ does it mean to us as people living with HIV? It means that our lives are at stake."

In Washington, activists from the Global AIDS Alliance try to deliver a mini ________ to the downtown office of Novartis.

07.

0206global

Concern About Global Warming

1 마음으로 듣기

- make for: ~을 만들다. 원인이 되다.
- brush off: (가볍게) 스치고 지나가다. 언급하다.
- those -ing: ~하는 (일반적인) 사람들
- s no different than ~ = is not any different from ~ (미국영어 구어체)

2 주어 듣기

_____ _______ ___________ on global warming finds ____ has begun and is very likely caused by man.

_____ _______ ___________ is being released Friday in Paris by hundreds of scientists.

_________ were dimmed on the Eiffel Tower to show concern about the environment.

_______ _________ _________ that's pushed across the Southeast is making travel difficult, stranding air passengers and closing schools in several states.

_____ ________ ______ _______, rain, and sleet have made for slippery roads and caused at least one traffic death in North Carolina.

_______ _________, the Vice President's daughter, is brushing off those criticizing her decision to have a baby with her lesbian partner.

Speaking at a Glamour magazine forum, Cheney says ____________ shows _____________________ raised by same-sex parents are no different than others.

▸ 주어(subject)는?

① 문장의 주요한 기능범주(functional category)의 하나로서 반드시 존재해야 한다.

② 명사구의 주요한 기능중의 하나이다.

③ 의미상으로 서술(predication)의 대상이다.

④ 시제문의 시제동사와 수와 인칭의 일치관계를 이룬다.

3 확장형

A new report on global warming finds _____ ______ begun and is very likely caused by man.

______ _________ report _____ _________ released Friday in Paris by hundreds of scientists.

____________ ________ dimmed on the Eiffel Tower to show concern about the environment.

The __________ _________ that's pushed across the Southeast _________ making travel difficult, stranding air passengers and closing schools in several states.

A mix of ________, rain, and sleet _______ _______ for slippery roads and caused at least one traffic death in North Carolina.

_________ ____________, the Vice President's daughter, __________ brushing off those criticizing her decision to have a baby with her lesbian partner.

Speaking at a Glamour magazine forum, Cheney says ____________ ________ ____________ ______________ by same-sex parents are no different than others.

4 연결음 듣기

A new report on global warming __________ _____ has begun and is very likely caused by man.

A key report is being released Friday in Paris by _____________ _____ scientists.

Lights were _____________ _____ the Eiffel Tower to show concern about the environment.

The winter storm that's ___________ ___________ the Southeast is making travel difficult, stranding air passengers and closing ____________ _____ several states.

A mix of snow, rain, and sleet have made for slippery roads and _________ ____ least one traffic death in North Carolina.

Mary Cheney, the Vice President's daughter, is _______________ _______ those criticizing her decision to ________ ____ baby with her lesbian partner.

______________ _____ a Glamour magazine forum, Cheney says research shows children raised by same-sex parents are no different than others.

▸ 가장 안 들리는 영어 단어는?

① 자신이 모르는 단어일까?

경험적으로 보면, 모르는 단어보다 알지만 (정확하게는 나중에야 알았지만) 그 문맥, 혹은 문장에서 쓰인 그 단어(의미)로 확인(identification)할 수 없어서 안들리는 단어이며, 이런 단어는 놀랍게도 대부분이 우리가 잘 알고 있는 일음절 단어들이다.

② 우리가 잘 아는 단어는 보통 수가 한정되어있고(폐쇄부류), 주로 문법적 기능을 하는 기능어(function word)에 속한다.

③ 기능어는 더 이상 외울 필요도 없으나 문장의 구조를 만들어가는 중요한 어휘이고, 알면서도 들리지 않으면 문장 전체의 내용을 해석할 수 없게 된다.

5 응용형

A new report on global warming finds it has __________ and is very likely caused by man.

A key report is being _______________ Friday in Paris by hundreds of scientists.

Lights were dimmed on the Eiffel Tower to show _________ about the environment.

The winter storm that's pushed across the Southeast is making travel difficult, ___________________ air passengers and ___________ schools in several states.

A mix of snow, rain, and sleet have made for slippery __________ and caused at least one traffic __________ in North Carolina.

Mary Cheney, the Vice President's daughter, is brushing off ________ criticizing her decision to have a baby with her lesbian partner.

Speaking at a Glamour magazine forum, Cheney says research shows children raised by same-sex ______________ are no different ________ others.

08. Republicans Block Iraq Debate

0207block

1 마음으로 듣기

▸ don = do on (=put on)
don disguise: 변복하다
doff = do off (=take off)

▸ non-binding resolution: 구속력이 없는 결의(안)

▸ count: 기소조항, 설명, 이유 등

2 시제동사 듣기

Senate Republicans _______ temporarily derailed plans to consider a non-binding resolution critical of President Bush's troop surge in Iraq.

Minority Leader Mitch McConnell ______ all resolutions ___________ be considered, not just one.

"We'_____ not trying to stop this debate."

"We ______ trying to structure it in a way that _____ fair to the competing voices in the Republican conference."

Democrats ______ the will of the voters on election day _____ being ignored.

An astronaut who _______ last July on a shuttle mission [was] arrested in Florida, charged with attempted kidnapping and other counts.

Navy Captain Lisa Nowak ________ disguise, Police ______, to confront a woman she ________________ _____ a rival for the affections of a space shuttle pilot.

▸ 시제동사는?
① 일반적인 문장(시제문/정형문)에서 시제가 표시되는 동사이다.
② 현재형과 과거형으로 나누어진다.
③ 주어 다음에 오는 조동사 혹은 본동사이다.
시제가 표시되지 않는 비시제문은 to-부정사구문이나 -ing 동명사구문, ing/-ed 분사형 구문 등이다.

3 확장형

Senate Republicans __________ temporarily ______________ plans to consider a non-binding resolution critical of President Bush's troop surge in Iraq.

Minority Leader Mitch McConnell says all resolutions _________ _____ ___________, not just one.

"We're not trying to stop this debate."

"We _______ ___________ to structure it in a way that ______ __________ to the competing voices in the Republican conference."

Democrats say the will of the voters on election day ______ _________ ignored.

An astronaut who ______ _______ _______ on a shuttle mission [was] arrested in Florida, charged with attempted kidnapping and other counts.

Navy Captain Lisa Nowak ________ _________, Police say, to confront a woman ________ ______________ is a rival for the affections of a space shuttle pilot.

▸ a woman (who/that) she believes [t] is a rival for the affections of a space shuttle pilot
(그녀가 우주왕복선 비행사의 사랑의 경쟁자라고 믿고 있는 한 여자)
관계절이 이중 내포구문의 구조를 가지고 있으며 선행사 NP [a woman]을 수식하고 있다.

4 연결음 듣기

Senate ____________ ______ temporarily derailed plans to consider a non-binding resolution _____________ ______ President Bush's troop surge in Iraq.

Minority Leader Mitch McConnell says all resolutions should be considered, not _____ ________.

"We're not trying to stop this debate."

"We are trying to structure it in a way _______ _____ fair to the competing voices __________ ________ Republican conference."

Democrats say the ________ ______ the voters on election day is being ignored.

An astronaut who flew last July on a shuttle mission [was] _______________ _____ Florida, charged with attempted kidnapping ________ ___________ counts.

Navy Captain Lisa Nowak donned disguise, _________ _____, to confront a woman she __________ _____ a rival for the affections of a space shuttle pilot.

▸ 기능어(function word)와 내용어(content word)는?

① 기능어는 주로 문법적 기능을 하는 어휘로서, 수도 제한되어 있는 폐쇄부류(closed- ended category)이다. (전치사, 접속사, 한정사, 대명사, 조동사 등)

② 내용어는 주로 어휘적 의미를 가지고 있으며, 수도 무제한으로 늘어날 수 있는 개방부류(open-ended category)이다. (명사, 동사, 형용사, 부사 등)

③ 기능어는 일음절 어휘가 많으며, 약화되거나 앞뒤 단어와 연결되어 발음의 변화를 가져오기 때문에 오히려 알아듣기가 어렵다는 것이 청취의 아이러니이다.

5 응용형

Senate Republicans have temporarily derailed _________ to consider a non-binding resolution critical of President Bush's troop surge in Iraq.

Minority Leader Mitch McConnell says all _____________ should be considered, not just one.

"We're not trying to stop _________ debate."

"We are trying to structure it in a way that is fair to the competing ___________ in the Republican conference."

Democrats say the will of the ____________ on election day is being ignored.

An astronaut who flew last July on a shuttle mission [was] arrested in Florida, __________________ with attempted kidnapping and other _____________.

Navy Captain Lisa Nowak donned disguise, Police say, to _____________ a woman she believes is a ___________ for the affections of a space shuttle pilot.

09. 0208hool

To Cope With Football Hooliganism

1 마음으로 듣기

▸ those (=people): 일반적인 사람들. 흔히 관계절의 선행사로 나타나거나, 후치수식절의 대상이 된다.
those [wanted for football violence]: 축구장 폭력으로 수배된 사람들
those [found guilty of violence]: 폭력의 유죄가 밝혀진 사람들
▸ behind closed doors: 관객없이, 문을 닫은 채로, 비밀로

2 접속사 듣기

The Italian Interior Minister Giuliano Amato said ________ ________ football matches are allowed to resume in Italy, they will have to be played behind closed doors ________________ the stadiums meet required safety standards.

He said ________ currently only 9 of the country's stadiums were considered safe.

Police powers will also be extended to cope with hooligans.

Christian Frazer reports from Rome.

"They promised drastic measures, _______ now they are telling the government has set out its tough proposals to deal with football hooliganism."

"Police will be given powers to arrest without warrant those wanted for football violence up to 48 hours after the crime."

"________ bans for those found guilty of violence at matches will now apply to under 18s as well."

"The Cabinet will meet again on Wednesday to put their proposals into a draft bill."

"They are promising they will be introduced immediately ______ be applied before next season."

▸ 접속사는?

① 동일하거나 유사한 구문의 좌우 연결어이다.

② 문장, 구, 단어 등을 연결한다.

③ 문장 연결어의 경우 등위접속사(coordinator)와 종속접속사(subordinator)로 나누어진다.

접속사는 동일구문이 연결된다는 면에서 문장 내부의 구조를 이해하는데 매우 중요한 단서가 된다. 'and'나 'or'는 일음절어로서 발음이 약화되는 것이 일반적이어서 앞 뒤 단어와 구별하기가 어려우므로 전체의 내용 및 앞 뒤 구조를 고려하여 판단해야 한다.

3 확장형

The Italian Interior Minister Giuliano Amato said that ________ __________ matches are allowed to resume in Italy, they will have to be played behind closed doors __________ __________ ____________ meet required safety standards.

He said that currently only 9 of the country's stadiums were considered safe.

Police powers will also be extended to cope with hooligans.

Christian Frazer reports from Rome.

"They promised drastic measures, ____________ ___________ they are telling the government has set out its tough proposals to deal with football hooliganism."

"Police will be given powers to arrest without warrant those wanted for football violence up to 48 hours after the crime."

"__________ ___________ for those found guilty of violence at matches will now apply to under 18s as well."

"The Cabinet will meet again on Wednesday to put their proposals into a draft bill."

"They are promising they will be introduced immediately ___________ _______ applied before next season."

▸ 접속사 'that'은?

① 연결어로서의 that은 다른 접속사와 구별되는 고유한 성질을 갖는다.

② 보문절(complement clause)의 머리어로서 보문자(complementizer)라 부르고, 그 보문절을 that-절이라 부른다.

③ 보문자 that은 엄격한 의미에서 문장의 연결어가 아니라 특정 범주와 그 보문절을 연결하는 역할을 한다.
e.g. I believe <u>that</u> John is innocent.
위 예문에서 보문자(COMP) 'that'은 문장 [I believe]와 문장 [John is innocent]의 연결어가 아니며, that-절은 주절동사 'believe'의 목적절(보충절/보문절)이다. 이 that-절을 believe의 내포절(embedded clause)이라 부른다.

④ 보문자 'that'은 어휘적인 의미가 없으며, 발음이 약화되거나 완전히 생략된다.

4 연결음 듣기

The Italian Interior Minister Giuliano Amato said that when football matches __________ ____________ ______ resume in Italy, they will have to be played behind closed doors unless the stadiums meet required safety standards.

He said that currently only 9 of the country's stadiums were considered safe.

Police powers will also be extended to ________ _______ hooligans.

Christian Frazer reports from Rome.

"They promised drastic measures, and now they are telling the _____________ _____ set _______ its tough proposals to deal with football hooliganism."

"Police will be given powers _______ __________ without warrant those wanted for football violence _______ _______ 48 hours after the crime."

"And bans for those found __________ _______ violence at matches will now apply to under 18s as well."

"The Cabinet will ______ _______ on Wednesday to put their proposals into a draft bill."

"They are promising ________ _______ be introduced immediately and be applied before next season."

▸ 형태소(morpheme)는?

① 단어를 만드는 의미의 최소단위(meaningful minimal unit)이다.

② 어휘적 의미를 가진 파생형태소(derivational morpheme)와 문법적 기능을 하는 굴절형태소(inflectional morpheme)로 나누어진다.

③ 파생형태소는 접두사(prefix)와 접미사(suffix)로 나누어지고 중복해서 부착될 수 있으나, 굴절형태소는 접미사인 어미로만 쓰고 중복될 수 없다.

④ 형태소의 첨가에 의해서 발음이나 억양의 변화를 가져오는 경우가 있다.

5 응용형

The Italian Interior Minister Giuliano Amato said that when football matches are __________________ to resume in Italy, they will have to be played behind ___________ doors unless the stadiums __________ required safety standards.

He said that currently only 9 of the country's stadiums were considered safe.

Police powers will also be _______________ to cope with hooligans.

Christian Frazer reports from Rome.

"They promised drastic ____________, and now they are telling the government has set out _______ tough proposals to deal with football hooliganism."

"Police will be given powers to arrest ________ warrant _______ wanted for football violence after 48 hours after the crime."

"And bans for _________ found guilty of violence at _____________ will now apply to under 18s as well."

"The Cabinet will meet again on Wednesday to put their ________________ into a draft bill."

"They are promising they will be introduced immediately and be _______ before next season."

10.

🖫0209hmong

The Fate Of The Hmong

1 마음으로 듣기

- the Hmong: 라오스와 접경지역에 사는 타일랜드의 소수민족
- ... about the fate of the group if they were returned to Laos.
  (만일 그들이 라오스로 돌려보내질 경우 그 단체의 운명(이 어떨는지에 대한) ...)
  if-절은 가정법이지만 주절 대신에 [about the fate of the group]이 온 드문 용법이다.
- trucks bound for neighboring Laos
  (이웃나라 라오스행 트럭)
  [bound for~]는 "...방향으로 가는/...행의" 형용사구로서 앞에 오는 'trucks'를 후치수식한다.

2 어휘동사 듣기

Government officials in Thailand _____ they will ________ the deportation of about 150 ethnic Hmong refugees after several Western countries _____________ to __________ accepting them for resettlement.

The United Nations Refugee Agency had ____________ expressed concern today about the fate of the group if they were ____________ to Laos.

The Thai Foreign Ministry spokesman _______ the Lao Hmong, many of whom are women and children, have been ____________ to an immigration detention center in the Northeastern Thai town of Nong Khai.

Scuffles were __________ out there earlier today when Thai officials __________ to _______ to ________ them into trucks bound for neighboring Laos.

▸ 어휘동사는?

① 본동사라 부르기도 하지만 동일한 것은 아니다.

② 독립적인 어휘적 의미를 갖는다는 면에서 조동사와 구분된다.

③ 시제문의 어휘동사는 조동사와 함께 쓰이며, 모든 조동사 다음에 온다.

④ 비시제문의 경우는 to-부정사구문의 'to' 다음에 원형으로 나오기도 하고, -ing 형, 혹은 -ed 형으로 나타기도 한다.

3 확장형

Government officials in Thailand say they ________ ___________ the deportation of about 150 ethnic Hmong refugees after several Western countries ___________ ______ consider accepting them for resettlement.

The United Nations Refugee Agency _____ __________ expressed concern today about the fate of the group if they ______ ___________ to Laos.

The Thai Foreign Ministry spokesman says the Lao Hmong, many of whom are women and children, _______ _______ __________ to an immigration detention center in the Northeastern Thai town of Nong Khai.

Scuffles ________ __________ ________ there earlier today when Thai officials began to try to ________ ________ into trucks bound for neighboring Laos.

▸ Be동사는?

① 본동사와 조동사로 사용되는 특별한 동사이다.

② 진행상(progressive aspect)과 수동태(passive voice)의 조동사로 쓰인다.

The company is seeking to overturn an Indian law.

Protesters were held in Washington.

③ 본동사로 쓰이며, 다른 조동사가 없으면 조동사로서 운용자가 된다.

This is thirteen years now.

4 연결음 듣기

Government officials in Thailand say __________ ________ delay the deportation ________ __________ 150 ethnic Hmong refugees after several Western countries agreed to consider accepting them for resettlement.

The United Nations Refugee Agency had conserved expressed concern today about the ________ ______ the group if they were returned to Laos.

The Thai Foreign Ministry spokesman says the Lao Hmong, many of whom are women and children, _______ _______ returned to an immigration detention center in the Northeastern Thai ________ ______ Nong Khai.

Scuffles were broken out there earlier today when Thai officials began to ________ ________ move them into trucks ____________ _______ neighboring Laos.

▸ 문장 안에서 약화되는 대표적인 발음은?

① 인칭대명사와 한정사
What's his name?
Ask him/her to come.
Bring an apple.

② 전치사
I'll see you at 10.
Thanks for coming.
I'm from Ulsan.
I've been waiting for 4 hours.

③ 접속사와 관계사
Come and see us.
He was tired but happy.
Do as you like.

④ 조동사
So am I.
They could do it.
What would you say?

5 응용형

Government officials in Thailand say they will delay the ______________ of about 150 ethnic Hmong ___________ after several Western countries agreed to consider accepting them for resettlement.

The United Nations Refugee Agency had conserved expressed ___________ today about the fate of the __________ if they were returned to Laos.

The Thai Foreign Ministry spokesman says the Lao Hmong, many of ________ are women and children, have been returned to an immigration _____________ center in the Northeastern Thai town of Nong Khai.

______________ were broken out there earlier today _______ Thai officials began to try to move them into trucks bound for neighboring Laos.

11. For The Environmental Crisis

0220crisis

1 마음으로 듣기

▸ class action lawsuit

[법률] 집단소송 (소비자 문제, 공해, 교통사고 따위로 인한 피해자들의 손해배상을 요구하는)

2 관사(a/the) 듣기

______ Dutch oil trading company has agreed to pay ________ nearly 200 million dollar settlement over a toxic spill that led to ______ major environmental crisis in ___________ Ivory Coast.

At least eight people were killed after _____ oil tanker dumped hundreds of tons of toxic waste in _______ Ivory Coast city of Abidjan.

Another 100,000 people sought medical treatment.

_______ company, Trafigura, says _______ payment is not admission of guilt.

Environmental groups including Greenpeace are calling _____ settlement inadequate.

_____ class action lawsuit on behalf of thousands of victims has been filed in Britain.

▸ 한정사와 관사의 차이는?

① 전통문법에서 일반적으로 사용되어온 용어로서의 관사(article)는 명사구의 맨 앞자리에 오는 대표적인 한정사이다.

② 부정관사(indefinite article) 'a(n)'과 정관사(definite article) 'the'는 그 용법이 매우 복잡하지만 뒤에 오는 머리어, 즉 명사의 의미와 화용론적 특성과 관련되어있다.

③ 부정관사는 명사가 비한정적이고 신정보인 경우에 쓰이고, 정관사는 명사가 한정적이고, 구정보인 경우에 쓰인다.

3 확장형

A Dutch oil trading company has agreed to pay a nearly 200 million dollar settlement over ____ ________ ________ that led to ____ ________ environmental crisis in the Ivory Coast.

At least eight people were killed after _____ ______ __________ dumped hundreds of tons of toxic waste in the Ivory Coast city of Abidjan.

Another 100,000 people sought medical treatment.

The company, Trafigura, says ______ _____________ is not admission of guilt.

Environmental groups including Greenpeace are calling ______ ___________inadequate.

_____ ___________ ____________ lawsuit on behalf of thousands of victims has been filed in Britain.

4 연결음 듣기

A Dutch oil trading company has agreed to pay a nearly 200 million dollar settlement ________ _____ toxic spill that ________ _____ a major environmental crisis in the Ivory Coast.

_____ __________ ___________ people were killed after an oil tanker dumped hundreds of tons of toxic waste in the Ivory Coast city of Abidjan.

Another 100,000 people sought medical treatment.

The company, Trafigura, says the payment is _______ admission of guilt.

Environmental groups including Greenpeace are calling the settlement inadequate.

A class action lawsuit on behalf of thousands of victims ______ _______ filed in Britain.

▸ 영어의 가장 힘이 센 (사용빈도가 높은) 발음은?

① 굴절형태소 '-s[s/z]'이다.

② 명사의 복수형의 발음으로 쓰인다. (dogs, desks, boys, ...)

③ 명사의 소유격의 발음으로 쓰인다. (father's, today's ...)

④ 시제동사의 현재시제표지로 쓰인다.

e.g. Tom goes to school today.

⑤ 연속되는 자음의 맨 앞에 오는 발음이다.

e.g. street, sprite, screw, slow, snow, smash

5 응용형

A Dutch oil trading company has agreed to pay a nearly 200 million dollar ______________ over a toxic spill that led to a major environmental _________ in the Ivory Coast.

At least eight people were killed after an oil tanker _________ hundreds of tons of toxic __________ in the Ivory Coast city of Abidjan.

Another 100,000 people ___________ medical treatment.

The company, Trafigura, says the payment is not _______________ of guilt.

Environmental groups including Greenpeace are calling the settlement __________.

A class action ___________ on behalf of thousands of victims has been filed in Britain.

12. Friendly Fire Killed A British Soldier

0210friendly

1 마음으로 듣기

- expletive: 무의미한 말, 알 수 없는 말, 허사
- (QUOTE): 기자가 인용부분이 바로 뒤에 오는 것을 알리기 위하여 가끔씩 사용하는 방송용 어구이다.
- *The Sun* released [what it claims [t] is the tape]:
  (*The Sun* 신문은 (자신들이) 그 (비디오) 테잎이라고 주장하는 것(what)을 발표[보도]하였다.)

2 전치사 듣기

British Lance Corporal Matty Hull was killed ________ a friendly fire incident outside Basra _______ the early days of the Iraq War.

Two U.S. A-10 Thunderbolts opened fire _______ Hull's tank on March 28, 2003.

"Ambassador, why didn't the Pentagon hold the tape?"

On Tuesday, the Ambassador to London did not respond _____ reporters' questions ________ a leaked gun camera video that caught the reactions and remorse _____ the 2 American pilots ______ tape.

But now U.S. military officials have agreed _______ release the cockpit recording, after it was published ______ a British tabloid.

The Sun released what it claims is the tape exchanged ____________ the pilots.

Pilot one says, "I'm gonna be sick," and pilot two responds _______ an expletive.

Then pilot one says, "Did you hear?," _______ which the second pilot responds _______ another expletive.

Finally, the first pilot says, (QUOTE) "We are ______ jail, dude."

According ______ *The Sun*'s transcript, the other pilot then weeps.

The Associated Press cannot confirm the authenticity ____ the tape or how *The Sun* gained possession ______ it.

An investigation _______ the U.S. Military did not result ______ a court martial, concluding that the firing was accidental.

3 확장형

British Lance Corporal Matty Hull was killed ________ _____ __________ fire incident outside Basra ______ ________ __________ days of the Iraq War.

Two U.S. A-10 Thunderbolts opened fire _____ ________ _______ on March 28, 2003.

"Ambassador, why didn't the Pentagon hold the tape?"

On Tuesday, the Ambassador to London did not respond to reporters'questions _____________ _____ leaked gun camera video that caught the reactions and remorse of the 2 American pilots ______ ________.

But now U.S. military officials have agreed _____ __________ the cockpit recording, after it was published by a British tabloid.

The Sun released what it claims is the tape exchanged _________________ _________ ____________.

Pilot one says, "I'm gonna be sick," and pilot two responds ______________ _____ _________________.

Then pilot one says, "Did you hear?," _____ _________ the second pilot responds with another expletive.

Finally, the first pilot says, (QUOTE) "We are ______ __________, dude."

_________________ ______ *The Sun*'s transcript, the other pilot then weeps.

The Associated Press cannot confirm the authenticity _______ _________ _________ or how *The Sun* gained possession of it.

An investigation by the U.S. Military did not result _________ _______ ____________ martial, concluding that the firing was accidental.

4 연결음 듣기

British Lance Corporal Matty Hull was killed during a friendly fire incident outside Basra in the early _________ _____ the Iraq War.

Two U.S. A-10 Thunderbolts opened fire on Hull's tank on March 28, 2003.

"Ambassador, why didn't the Pentagon hold the tape?"

On Tuesday, the __________ _____ London did not respond to reporters'questions about a leaked gun camera video that ___________ _______ reactions and remorse of the 2 American pilots on tape.

But now U.S. military officials ______ __________ to release the cockpit recording, __________ _____ _______ published by a British tabloid.

The Sun released what it __________ _____ the tape exchanged between the pilots.

Pilot one says, "I'm gonna be sick," and pilot two responds with an expletive.

Then _________ ______ says, "Did you hear?," to which the second pilot responds with another expletive.

Finally, the first pilot says, (QUOTE) "We are in jail, dude."

According to *The Sun*'s transcript, the other pilot then weeps.

The Associated Press cannot confirm the authenticity of the tape or how *The Sun* gained possession ______ ______.

An investigation by the U.S. Military _____ _____ result in a court martial, concluding that the firing was accidental.

5 응용형

British Lance Corporal Matty Hull was ________________ during a friendly fire ________________ outside Basra in the early days of the Iraq War.

Two U.S. A-10 Thunderbolts ___________ fire on Hull's tank on March 28, 2003.

"Ambassador, why didn't the Pentagon ________ the tape?"

On Tuesday, the _____________ to London did not respond to reporters'questions about a _______________ gun camera video that caught the reactions and _________ of the 2 American pilots on tape.

But now U.S. military officials have agreed to release the ________ recording, after it was published by a British tabloid.

The Sun released what it claims is the tape ________________ between the pilots.

Pilot one says, "I'm gonna be sick," and pilot two responds with an expletive.

Then pilot one says, "Did you hear?," to which the second pilot responds with another __________________.

Finally, the first pilot says, (QUOTE) "We are in jail, dude."

According to *The Sun*'s transcript, the other pilot then _____________.

The Associated Press cannot confirm the authenticity of the tape or how *The Sun* ______________ possession of it.

An investigation by the U.S. Military did not result in a court martial, _____________ that the firing was accidental.

13. Birds Began Dying

0214bird

1 마음으로 듣기

- premises: 건물이 딸린 토지, 구역, 구내 (복수형에 유의)
- has been contained: 봉쇄(통제)되었다
- discover if(=whether) ~: ...인지 아닌지를 찾아내다

2 접속사(관계사 포함) 듣기

In the sheds of Europe's largest turkey producer outside of London, birds began dying this week.

Tonight the farm is sealed off, Police ensuring there is no movement ______ no possibility the virus will spread.

"No birds have left the premises _______ no product has left the premises. _____ so the disease on that premises has been contained."

Laboratory test today confirmed the killer virus was H5N1.

That's the virus ______ spread from South Asia to Africa and Russia, and last year arrived in Europe.

In 4 years, more than 160 people _____ caught the virus have died, most of them in Asia.

Scientists fear it could mutate into something more easily transmitted to humans.

That hasn't happened.

For officials now, the top priority is to discover _____ other birds are sick ______ _____ there is a risk of further spreading.

▸ 보문자 'that'은?

① 타동사의 목적절을 인도한다.

Scientists fear (that) it could ....

② 관계절을 인도한다.

That's the virus that spread from South Africa ...

③ 동격절을 인도한다.

There is no possibility (that) the virus will spread.

3 확장형

In the sheds of Europe's largest turkey producer outside of London, birds began dying this week.

Tonight the farm is sealed off, Police ensuring there is no movement ____________ ________ possibility the virus will spread.

"No birds have left the premises ________ ________ product has left the premises. ________ ________ the disease on that premises has been contained."

Laboratory test today confirmed the killer virus was H5N1.

That's the virus ________ ____________ from South Asia to Africa and Russia, __________ _________ _________ arrived in Europe.

In 4 years, more than 160 people _______ ___________ the virus have died, most of them in Asia.

Scientists fear it could mutate into something more easily transmitted to humans.

That hasn't happened.

For officials now, the top priority is to discover _____ ________ birds are sick and _____ _________ is a risk of further spreading.

▸ 영어의 가장 힘이 약한 발음은?

① 중립음(schwa) [ə]이다.

② [ə]는 강세가 없는 거의 모든 모음의 발음으로 나타난다.

e.g. about, admit, allow, boxes, twentieth 등

③ 약화된 발음의 대표형이지만 다른 발음과 이어지면 다시 살아난다.

4 연결음 듣기

In the ______ ____ Europe's largest turkey producer outside of London, birds began dying this week.

Tonight the farm is sealed off, Police ensuring ________ _____ no movement and no possibility the virus will spread.

"No birds have left the premises and no product has left the premises. And so the disease on that premises has been contained."

Laboratory test today _________________ _______ killer virus was H5N1.

That's the virus that spread from South Asia to Africa and Russia, and last year ____________ ____ Europe.

In 4 years, more than 160 people who caught the virus have died, _________ ____ _______ _____ Asia.

Scientists fear ____ __________ mutate into something more easily transmitted to humans.

That hasn't happened.

For officials now, the top priority is to discover if other birds are sick and if there ______ _____ risk of further spreading.

5 응용형

In the sheds of Europe's largest turkey __________ outside of London, birds began dying this week.

Tonight the farm is __________ off, Police ensuring there is no movement and no possibility the virus will spread.

"No birds have left the ____________ and no product has left the premises. And so the disease on that premises has been ________________."

____________________ test today confirmed the killer virus was H5N1.

That's the virus that spread from South Asia _____ Africa and Russia, and last year arrived in Europe.

In 4 years, more than 160 people who caught the ______ have died, most of them in Asia.

Scientists fear it could _____________ into something more easily transmitted to humans.

That hasn't happened.

For officials now, the top ____________ is to discover if other birds are sick and if there is a risk of ____________ spreading.

14.

0219snow

Heavy Snow In New York

1 마음으로 듣기

- a wind chill factor: 풍속냉각지수 (=a wind chill index)
- 상황묘사 소절(small clause): <with+ 주어 + 술어> 소절구문
  with [another quick blast of snow] [expected]
  (또 한차례의 쾌속 눈보라가 예상되는 가운데)
  with [a wind chill factor] [dropping ...]
  (찬바람 요인이 ... 떨어트릴 상황에서)
- be due to + V ...: ~할 예정이다

2 수식어(부사구) 듣기

It's beyond a winter wonderland, and ______ parts of New York are starting to face serious problems.

More than 100 inches of snow has ____________ fallen, and forecasters continue to predict the frigid outlook.

Central New York buried.

Parts of the region _________________ covered, where all you can see is this.

And with another quick blast of snow expected, New York's Governor has declared a State disaster emergency.

Crews are working hard to at least keep the streets clear, but the task is ________ overwhelming, _________________ since it's hard to even get _____________.

Part of the problem _______?

There's ____________ to put all the snow.

Some snow plow drivers have been given permission to dump loads of snow into open water such as lakes and rivers.

That might cause a problem when the snow melts in the spring, ________________ creating localized flooding.

New York could be facing problems from months to come.

What's worse, temperatures are due to dip to 11 degrees with a wind chill factor dropping to minus five below.

For many residents, all they can do is try to keep ahead of the pile-up and look to forecasters to predict warmer temperatures.

3 확장형

It's beyond a winter wonderland, and ______ ________ of New York are starting to face serious problems.

More than 100 inches of snow _____ _________ _______, and forecasters continue to predict the frigid outlook.

Central New York buried.

Parts of the region ________________ __________, where all you can see is this.

And with another quick blast of snow expected, New York's Governor has declared a State disaster emergency.

Crews are working hard to at least keep the streets clear, but the task ________ ____________ overwhelming, especially since it's hard to even ______ __________.

Part of the problem now?

___________ ____________ to put all the snow.

Some snow plow drivers have been given permission to dump loads of snow into open water such as lakes and rivers.

That might cause a problem when the snow melts in the spring, ________________ ______________ localized flooding.

New York could be facing problems from months to come.

What's worse, temperatures are due to dip to 11 degrees with a wind chill factor dropping to minus five below.

For many residents, all they can do is try to keep ahead of the pile-up and look to forecasters to predict warmer temperatures.

4 연결음 듣기

It's beyond a winter wonderland, _______ _______ parts of New York are starting to face serious problems.

More than 100 inches of snow has officially fallen, and forecasters continue to ______________ _______ frigid outlook.

Central New York buried.

___________ ______ the region completely covered, where all you can see is this.

_________ ________ another quick blast of snow expected, New York's _________ ___________ declared a State disaster emergency.

Crews are working hard to at least keep the streets clear, but the task is clearly overwhelming, especially since it's _________ _____ even get anywhere.

Part of the problem now?

There's nowhere to put all the snow.

Some snow plow drivers ______ _______ given permission to dump loads of snow into open water such as __________ _______ rivers.

That might cause a problem when the snow __________ _____ the spring, possibly creating localized flooding.

New York could be facing problems from months to come.

What's worse, temperatures are _______ _____ dip to 11 degrees with a wind chill factor dropping to minus five below.

For many residents, all they can do is try to _______ _________ _____ the pile-up and look to forecasters to predict warmer temperatures.

5 응용형

It's beyond a winter wonderland, and now parts of New York are ________ to face serious problems.

More than 100 inches of snow has officially fallen, and forecasters continue to predict the __________ outlook.

Central New York buried.

Parts of the region completely covered, __________ all you can see is this.

And with another quick _________ of snow expected, New York's Governor has _____________ a State disaster emergency.

__________ are working hard to at least keep the streets clear, but the _______ is clearly overwhelming, especially since it's hard to even get anywhere.

Part of the problem now?

There's nowhere to put all the snow.

Some snow plow drivers have been given permission to _______ loads of snow into open water such as lakes and rivers.

That might cause a problem ______ the snow melts in the spring, possibly creating localized flooding.

New York could be facing problems from months to come.

What's worse, temperatures are due to dip to 11 degrees with a wind chill ___________ dropping to minus five below.

For many residents, all they can do is try to keep ahead of the ____________ and look to forecasters to predict ____________ temperatures.

15. Free Hug Campaign

🖫0118hug

1 마음으로 듣기

▸ the one feeling: 하나가 되는 느낌

2 한정사 듣기

Need _____ hug?

It's not always _____ easy thing to find in ______ heart of ______ cold-hearted city.

_____ group of students were handing them out for free on _____ streets of Seoul, South Korea, recently.

They were inspired by ______ free hugs campaign started in Australia two years ago.

"친구가 안기자길래 같이 안겼는데... "

________ young woman says ______ friend suggested she hug ____ stranger.

She says she liked _______ one feeling and decided this is ____ good movement.

Hug givers carry ____ sign advertizing _________ service.

Interested?

Just come on over and start squeezing.

______ hugs may be free, but that doesn't mean ______ huggers don't get anything in return.

______ idea behind ______ campaign?

To engage in random acts of kindness.

3 확장형

Need _____ ______?

It's not always ______ ________ _________ to find in _______ __________ _____ the cold-hearted city.

_____ ___________ ______ students were handing them out for free _______ _______ ______________ of Seoul, South Korea, recently.

They were inspired by the free hugs campaign started in Australia two years ago.

"친구가 안기자길래 같이 안겼는데... "

This young woman says _______ ________ suggested she hug _____ ____________.

She says she liked _______ ______ _________ and decided this is a good movement.

Hug givers carry a sign advertizing _________ ____________.

Interested?

Just come on over and start squeezing.

______ ________ may be free, but that doesn't mean _____ ___________ don't get anything in return.

_______ _________ behind the campaign?

To engage in random acts of kindness.

4 연결음 듣기

_________ _____ hug?

It's not always an easy thing _____ _______ in the ________ _____ the cold-hearted city.

A _________ _____ students were handing them out for free on the streets of Seoul, South Korea, recently.

They were inspired by the free hugs campaign ________ _____ Australia two years ago.

"친구가 안기자길래 같이 안겼는데... "

This young woman says her friend suggested she ________ _____ stranger.

She says she liked the one feeling _______ ____________ this is a good movement.

Hug givers carry a sign advertizing their service.

Interested?

Just come on ________ _______ start squeezing.

The hugs may be free, but that doesn't mean the huggers don't get anything in return.

The idea behind the campaign?

To engage in random acts of kindness.

5 응용형

Need a _______?

It's not always an easy thing to find in the heart of the ________________ city.

A group of students were ________ them out for free on the streets of Seoul, South Korea, recently.

They were __________ by the free hugs campaign started in Australia two years ago.

"친구가 안기자길래 같이 안겼는데... "

This young woman says her friend suggested she _______ a stranger.

She says she liked the _______ feeling and decided this is a good movement.

Hug givers carry a _______ advertizing their service.

Interested?

Just come on over and start _______________.

The hugs may be free, but that doesn't mean the huggers don't get _________ in return.

The idea __________ the campaign?

To engage in random ________ of kindness.

Part 2

Practical Guides to the Current English Listening Skill

…01.

0101vitamin

Vitamin D

1 마음으로 듣기

▸ multiple sclerosis: 다발성 경화증(M.S.)

2 한정사 듣기

Vitamin D is found in milk and sunlight, and ____ new study suggests it may help prevent multiple sclerosis.

Researchers found that certain people with ______ highest levels of vitamin D in ____________ blood were 62 percent less likely to develop M.S..

Doctors say more study is needed to confirm ________ results, but hope ________ finding leads to _____ better understanding of ________ disease.

▸ 한정사(determiner)는?

① 명사구(noun phrase)의 맨 앞에 오는 지정어(specifier)이다.

② 머리어(head)인 명사의 구체적인 자질을 지정해주는 기능범주이며, 머리어와 수의 일치를 이룬다.

e.g. a good boy / two good boys, this book / these books

③ 한정사는 관사(a(n), the)), 지시형용사(this, that, these, those), 수나 양을 표현하는 양화사(each, every, any, some, all, several, many, much, more), 소유형용사(my, our, his, her, its, our, their) 및 모든 명사구(NP)의 소유격 표현 등이 있다.

3 확장형

Vitamin D is found in milk and sunlight, and _____ ________ __________ suggests it may help prevent multiple sclerosis.

Researchers found that certain people with ________ __________ levels of vitamin D in __________ _______________ were 62 percent less likely to develop M.S..

Doctors say more study is needed to confirm __________ _____________, but hope ________ _____________ leads to a better understanding of _______ _____________.

▸ 청취력은 예측력/추리력/눈치력이 절반?

여러분이 미국인 친구에게 이렇게 물었다고 하자. “How old is your father?” 친구의 대답은 기대와 달리 아주 짧게, 그것도 빠르게 나왔다. “Fiftee-.” 평소에도 숫자를 영어로 알아듣는데 어려움이 있던 터라 바로 머리에 들어오지 않았다. “15 세야, 50 세야?” 이때 여러분의 머리는 번개처럼 움직인다. 그 결과 저 친구가 한말은 “Fifteen.”이 아니고 “Fifty.” 임이 분명하다고 결론을 내린다. (그 이유는 여러분이 더 잘 안다!) 이러한 무의식적인 인지능력은 청취력에서도 엄청난 위력을 발휘한다. 더 정확히 말하면 이 능력을 최대한도로 활용하느냐가 여러분의 청취력을 결정한다고 해도 과언이 아니다. 여러분이 지금부터 직접 체험해보시길 바란다.

4 연결음 듣기

Vitamin D is ________ _____ milk and sunlight, and a new study suggests ________ ________ help prevent multiple sclerosis.

Researchers found that certain people with the highest ____________ _____ vitamin D in their blood were 62 percent less __________ ______ develop M.S..

Doctors say more ___________ _____ needed to confirm the results, but hope the finding leads to a better understanding ______ _______ disease.

▸ 영어의 자음(consonant)은?

① 유성음과 무성음으로 나누어진다.

② 모음(vowel)의 앞과 뒤에 놓여 음절을 구성하며, 자음이 연속 나오기도 한다.
   e.g. strike, West Bank

③ 단어의 끝에 오면 귀에 들리지 않을 정도로 약하게 발음되지만(unreleased), 그 뒤에 모음이 오면 다시 음이 살아나서 그 모음과 연결될 수도 있다.

5 응용형

Vitamin D is found in ________ and sunlight, and a new study suggests it may help ___________ multiple sclerosis.

Researchers found that certain people ______ the highest levels of vitamin D in their blood ________ 62 percent less likely to develop M.S..

Doctors say more study is needed to ___________ the results, but hope the finding ___________ to a better understanding of the disease.

▸ 문장 안에서 약화되는 대표적인 발음은?

① 인칭대명사와 한정사

What's <u>his</u> name?
Ask <u>him/her</u> to come.
Bring <u>an</u> apple.

② 전치사

I'll see you <u>at</u> 10.
Thanks <u>for</u> coming.
I'm <u>from</u> Ulsan.
I've been waiting <u>for</u> 4 hours.

③ 접속사와 관계사

Come <u>and</u> see us.
He was tired <u>but</u> happy.
Do as you like.

④ 조동사

So <u>am</u> I.
They <u>could</u> do it.
What <u>would</u> you say?

02. France Has A New President

0516France

1 마음으로 듣기

- runoff election: 결선투표
- the *Arc de Triomphe*: 프랑스 파리의 개선문(외래어를 이탤릭으로 씀)
- artillary salutes: 포병대의 예포

  as artillery salutes echoed outside

  (포병대의 예포가 밖에서 울려퍼질 때)

2 어휘동사 듣기

Nicolas Sarkozy has been officially ____________ as the new President of France.

Outgoing President Jacques Chirac ____________ his successor with the codes for France's nuclear arsenal as artillery salutes __________ outside.

Mr. Sarkozy _____ to _____ to the *Arc de Triomphe* to rekindle the flame on the tomb of the unknown soldier before taking a brief trip to Berlin to meet German Chancellor Angela Merkel.

Mr. Sarkozy will __________ to France and ____________ his Cabinet tomorrow or Friday.

Mr. Sarkozy _______ Socialist candidate Segolene Royal in a runoff election on May 6.

Britain's outgoing Prime Minister Tony Blair ___________ in Washington later today for talks at the White House with President Bush.

Mr. Blair's meetings with Mr. Bush today and tomorrow will ____ his last as Britain's Head of State.

▸ 어휘동사는?

① 본동사라 부르기도 하지만 동일한 것은 아니다.
② 독립적인 어휘적 의미를 갖는다는 면에서 조동사와 구분된다.
③ 시제문의 어휘동사는 조동사와 함께 쓰이며, 모든 조동사 다음에 온다.
④ 비시제문의 경우는 to-부정사구문의 'to' 다음에 원형으로 나오기도 하고, -ing 형으로 나타기도 한다.

3 확장형

Nicolas Sarkozy has been __________ __________ as the new President of France.

Outgoing President Jacques Chirac ___________ _____ successor with the codes for France's nuclear arsenal as artillery salutes __________ __________.

Mr. Sarkozy _____ _____ _____ to the *Arc de Triomphe* to rekindle the flame on the tomb of the unknown soldier before taking a brief trip to Berlin to meet German Chancellor Angela Merkel.

Mr. Sarkozy _____ __________ to France and ___________ ______ Cabinet tomorrow or Friday.

Mr. Sarkozy beat Socialist candidate Segolene Royal in a runoff election on May 6.

Britain's outgoing Prime Minister Tony Blair _________ ____ Washington later today for talks at the White House with President Bush.

Mr. Blair's meetings with Mr. Bush today and tomorrow ______ ____ his last as Britain's Head of State.

▸ Be동사는?

① 본동사와 조동사로 사용되는 특별한 동사이다.

② 진행상(progressive aspect)과 수동태(passive voice)의 조동사로 쓰인다.
The company is seeking to overturn an Indian law.
Protesters were held in Washington.

③ 본동사로 쓰이며, 다른 조동사가 없으면 조동사로서 운용자가 된다.
This is thirteen years now.

4 연결음 듣기

Nicolas Sarkozy has been officially inaugurated as the new ________________ ________ France.

Outgoing President Jacques Chirac presented his successor _______ ______ codes for France's nuclear arsenal as artillery salutes ____________ __________.

Mr. Sarkozy is to go to the *Arc de Triomphe* to rekindle the flame on the tomb _______ _______ unknown soldier before taking a brief ________ _____ Berlin to meet German Chancellor Angela Merkel.

Mr. Sarkozy will ____________ _______ France and appoint his Cabinet tomorrow or Friday.

Mr. Sarkozy beat Socialist candidate Segolene Royal in a runoff election on May 6.

Britain's outgoing Prime Minister Tony Blair _________ ____ Washington later today for talks at the White House with President Bush.

Mr. Blair's meetings with Mr. Bush today and tomorrow will be his last as Britain's _________ ______ State.

▸ 영어의 모음은?

① 음절의 핵(nucleus)이다. 따라서 모음의 수는 음절의 수와 같다.

② 강세(stress)가 주어진다.

③ 단어의 경계를 넘어서 앞뒤 자음과 연결음이 될 수 있다.

5 응용형

Nicolas Sarkozy has been officially inaugurated ______ the new President of France.

Outgoing President Jacques Chirac presented his successor with the _________ for France's nuclear arsenal as artillery _____________ echoed outside.

Mr. Sarkozy is to go to the *Arc de Triomphe* to ___________ the flame on the tomb of the _____________ soldier before taking a brief trip to Berlin to meet German Chancellor Angela Merkel.

Mr. Sarkozy will return to France and appoint his Cabinet tomorrow ______ Friday.

Mr. Sarkozy beat Socialist candidate Segolene Royal in a _______ election on May 6.

Britain's outgoing Prime Minister Tony Blair arrives in Washington later today for _______ at the White House ________ President Bush.

Mr. Blair's meetings with Mr. Bush today and tomorrow will be his ________ as Britain's Head of State.

03.

0622missing

A Missing Woman And A Baby

1 마음으로 듣기

- the umbilical cord: 탯줄
- her due day: 출산 예정일

2 접속사(관계사 포함) 듣기

There may be a bizarre twist in the case of a pregnant Ohio mother ___________ disappeared, _______ it could be just coincidence.

About 45 miles away from ________ 26-year old Jessie Davis vanished, a newborn baby was found in a basket on a doorstep.

Investigators say the infant girl was newly born _______ the umbilical cord was still attached.

DNA samples are now being taken to see ______ there is any connection with the missing pregnant woman.

According to relatives, Jessie Davis was expecting a girl _____ her due day was July 3.

________ her mother arrived at the house _______ found Davis missing last week, it was also determined her cell phone _______ a comforter had been taken.

Police have questioned the father of Davis's unborn girl ______ also is the father of her 2-year-old son.

Police patrolman Bobby Cutts Jr. is estranged from his wife.

Investigators say Cutts has been cooperative ______ that they have no suspects at this time.

▸ 접속사는?

① 동일하거나 유사한 구문의 좌우 연결어이다.

② 문장, 구, 단어 등을 연결한다.

③ 문장 연결어의 경우 등위접속사(coordinator)와 종속접속사(subordinator)로 나누어진다.

접속사는 동일구문이 연결된다는 면에서 문장 내부의 구조를 이해하는데 매우 중요한 단서가 된다. 'and'나 'or'는 일음절어로서 발음이 약화되는 것이 일반적이어서 앞 뒤 단어와 구별하기가 어려우므로 전체의 내용 및 앞 뒤 구조를 고려하여 판단해야 한다.

3 확장형

There may be a bizarre twist in the case of a pregnant Ohio mother __________ ____________, or it could be just coincidence.

About 45 miles away from ______ _______ old Jessie Davis vanished, a newborn baby was found in a basket on a doorstep.

Investigators say the infant girl was newly born _______ _____ _________ cord was still attached.

DNA samples are now being taken to see _____ _______ is any connection with the missing pregnant woman.

According to relatives, Jessie Davis was expecting a girl _____ _____ due day was July 3.

_______ ______ _________ arrived at the house and found Davis missing last week, it was also determined her cell phone _____ ____ _________ had been taken.

Police have questioned the father of Davis's unborn girl _____ ______ is the father of her 2-year-old son.

Police patrolman Bobby Cutts Jr. is estranged from his wife.

Investigators say Cutts has been cooperative _____ ______ they have no suspects at this time.

4 연결음 듣기

There may be a bizarre twist in the case of a pregnant Ohio mother who disappeared, or _____ __________ _____ just coincidence.

About 45 miles away from where 26-year old Jessie Davis vanished, a newborn baby was _________ _____ a basket on a doorstep.

Investigators say the infant girl was newly born and the umbilical cord __________ ____________ attached.

DNA ____________ _____ now being taken to see if there is any connection with the missing pregnant woman.

According to relatives, Jessie Davis was expecting a girl and her due day was July 3.

When her mother arrived at the house and found Davis missing _______ _______, _____ _______ also determined her cell phone and a comforter had been taken.

Police have questioned the father of Davis's unborn girl who also is the father _______ _______ 2-year-old son.

Police patrolman Bobby Cutts Jr. is estranged from his wife.

Investigators say Cutts has been cooperative and that they have no ____________ _____ this time.

▸ 발음(pronunciation/sound)과 철자(spelling/letter)의 관계는?

① 발음은 선사시대부터, 철자는 유사시대 이후에 생겼다.

② 발음은 시간 언어, 철자는 공간언어이다.

③ 발음과 철자는 일치할 수 없고, 발음기호조차도 실제 발음과 같을 수 없다.

5 응용형

There may be a __________ twist in the case of a pregnant Ohio mother who disappeared, or it could be just __________________.

About 45 miles away from where 26-year old Jessie Davis __________, a newborn baby was found in a basket on a doorstep.

Investigators say the ________ girl was newly born and the umbilical cord was still attached.

DNA samples are now being taken to see if there is any connection with the ______________ pregnant woman.

According to relatives, Jessie Davis was expecting a girl and her due _____ was July 3.

When her mother arrived at the house and _______ Davis missing last week, it was also ________________ her cell phone and a comforter had been taken.

Police have _____________ the father of Davis's unborn girl who also is the father of her 2-year-old son.

Police patrolman Bobby Cutts Jr. is ______________ from his wife.

Investigators say Cutts has been _______________ and that they have no suspects at this time.

04.

0611bill

Embryonic Stem Cell Research

1 마음으로 듣기

▸ daring him to veto it again: 다시 거부하려면 해보라고 그에게 도전하면서

▸ embryonic stem cell research [which scientists say [t] has enormous potential]
([과학자들이 거대한 잠재력을 가지고 있다고 말하는] 배아줄기세포 연구)
이중 내포구문으로서 'which'는 주격 관계사이다.

2 대명사 듣기

Embryonic Stem Cell Research?

President Bush considers that immoral, and ______ can't sell human embryos even for research on possible cures for diseases and disabilities.

But Congress again defied the President.

_________ sent ______ pretty much the same bill _____ vetoed last year, daring ____________ to veto _____ again.

______ 's a bill that would allow Federal funding to support embryonic stem cell research which scientists say has enormous potential - the possibility to help diabetes, Parkinson's, cancer, even spinal cord injuries.

The measure had strong public support.

_____ passed by large margins in the House and Senate.

But _____ fell short of the two-thirds needed to override the veto, and the President says ______ will veto ______ again.

▸ 대명사(pronoun)는?

① 선행하는 명사구를 대신하는 기능범주 이다.

② 선행사와 성, 수 등이 일치한다.

③ 일음절인 경우가 많아서 소리가 약해지기 쉽고, 주위음의 영향을 받기 쉽다.

④ 인칭대명사, 지시대명사, 부정대명사, 재귀대명사, 의문대명사, 관계대명사 등 다양하고 쉽지 않은 용법을 가지고 있으므로 문맥에서 그 용법을 주의 깊게 관찰하는 것이 좋다.

3 확장형

Embryonic Stem Cell Research?

President Bush considers that immoral, and _____ ______ sell human embryos even for research on possible cures for diseases and disabilities.

But Congress again defied the President.

_________ _______ him pretty much the same bill he vetoed last year, daring __________ _____ ________ it again.

_______ _____ _______ that would allow Federal funding to support embryonic stem cell research which scientists say has enormous potential – the possibility to help diabetes, Parkinson's, cancer, even spinal cord injuries.

The measure had strong public support.

_____ __________ by large margins in the House and Senate.

But ______ ________ short of the two-thirds needed to override the veto, and the President says ______ _______ veto it again.

4 연결음 듣기

Embryonic Stem Cell Research?

President Bush considers that immoral, _______ _______ can't sell human embryos even for research on possible cures for __________ ______ disabilities.

But Congress again ___________ ______ President.

They sent him pretty much the same bill he vetoed last year, daring ________ ____ veto it again.

It's a bill that __________ ________ Federal funding to support embryonic stem cell research which scientists say has enormous potential – the possibility to help diabetes, Parkinson's, cancer, even spinal cord injuries.

The ___________ ______ strong public support.

_____ __________ by large margins in the House and Senate.

But it fell ______ ____ the two-thirds needed to override the veto, and the President says he will veto it again.

▸ 가장 짧은 영어 단어는?

① 하나의 모음으로 만들어진 'a'이다.

② 자음(C)과 모음(V)이 교차하여 만들어진 단어가 가장 자연스러우나, 대부분의 단어는 이러한 배열을 가지고 있지 않다.

(C)(C)(C)V(C)(C)(C)

e.g. strike, scream, splash / prompt, distinct, glimpse, jinx, text, midst

③ 단어의 경계를 넘어서면 연결음은 더욱 길어지고 복잡해진다.

e.g. ice cream / I scream / iced tea

5 응용형

Embryonic Stem Cell Research?

President Bush considers that __________, and you can't sell human embryos even for research on possible ___________ for diseases and disabilities.

But Congress again _________ the President.

They sent him pretty much the same bill he vetoed last year, ________ him to veto it again.

It's a bill that would allow Federal funding to support embryonic stem cell research _________ scientists say has enormous ____________ – the possibility to help diabetes, Parkinson's, cancer, even spinal cord injuries.

The measure had strong public support.

It passed by large _____________ in the House and Senate.

But it fell short of the two-thirds needed to _________ the veto, and the President says he will veto it again.

05.

0109diet

Reading About Diet

1 마음으로 듣기

▸ be more likely to V ~: ...할 가능성이 더 높다

... were more likely, 5 years down the road, to practice extreme weight loss measures ... (5년 동안 계속해서, 극단적인 체중감량조치를 실천할 가능성이 ...보다 더 높았다)

▸ 5 years down the road: 계속해서 5년동안 (여기서는 5년의 연구기간 동안 계속해서)

2 주어 명사구 듣기

_____ _______ _________ suggests _________ about diet and weight loss could have unhealthy consequences for young girls.

_____ University of Minnesota _______ found that _________ ______ who frequently read magazine articles about dieting were more likely, 5 years down the road, to practice extreme weight loss measures such as vomiting than girls who never read such articles.

_____ apparently doesn't seem to matter whether ______ ________ were overweight when ________ started reading about weight loss, or whether ________ considered their weight important.

▸ 주어 명사구는?

① 주어로 쓰이는 명사구이다.

② 고유명사나 대명사도 넓은 의미의 명사구이다.

③ 주어 명사구는 시제동사와 수와 인칭의 일치가 되어야 한다.

e.g. [A new study] [suggests] ...

[New studies] [suggest] ...

3 확장형

A new study suggests __________ about diet and weight loss ___________ ______ unhealthy consequences for young girls.

_____ University of Minnesota ________ ________ that __________ _______ who frequently read magazine articles about dieting ______ more likely, 5 years down the road, to practice extreme weight loss measures such as vomiting than girls who never read such articles.

It apparently doesn't seem to matter whether _____ _________ ______ overweight when _______ ___________ reading about weight loss, or whether they considered their weight important.

▸ 직청직해의 단서는?

① 시간적 순서(Expressions of Time Order)
First, Second, Then, Last, Finally, Before, After

② 관점의 이동(Transitional Markers)
Therefore, And, Then, However, on the contrary, otherwise, Though

③ 예시(Showing examples)
For example, For instance, Take for instance, Let's say, In our example

④ 화제의 변경(Change of Topics)
As for, Speaking of, By the way, In addition (to)

4 연결음 듣기

A new study suggests reading about _______ _____ weight loss could have unhealthy consequences for young girls.

A _______________ ______ Minnesota study found that teenage girls who frequently ____________ _________________ articles about dieting were more likely, 5 years down the road, ____ _________ extreme weight loss measures _______ _____ vomiting than girls who never read such articles.

______ __________________ doesn't seem to matter whether the girls were ________________ _________ they started reading about _________ _______, or whether they considered their weight important.

▸ 가장 긴 영어 단어는?

① SmileS
시작과 끝이 'mile'이나 되니까. (humor!)

② 이론적으로 가장 긴 단어도 없고, 가장 긴 문장도 없다.

③ 이유는 아무리 길어도 거기에다 다시 더 긴 단어나 문장을 만들 수 있기 때문이다. 같은 이유로 단어의 수나 문장의 수도 그 생성규칙에 따라 무한정 늘어날 수 있다.

5 응용형

A new study suggests reading about diet and weight loss could have ____________ consequences for young girls.

A University of Minnesota study found that teenage girls ________ frequently read magazine articles about ________ were more likely, 5 years down the road, to practice extreme weight loss _____________ such as vomiting than girls _______ never read such articles.

It apparently doesn't seem to matter _________ the girls were overweight when they started reading about weight loss, or whether they considered their ____________ important.

▸ 부사 수식어는?

① 주로 동사와 형용사를 수식한다.
② 형용사처럼 비교급과 최상급을 갖는다.
③ 형용사와 동일한 형태를 갖거나, 형용사에 '–ly' 접미사를 부착하여 부사를 만든다.
④ '–ly' 부사형의 경우에 형용사가 [t], [d]로 끝나는 발음이면 부사의 발음도 하기나 듣기나 모두 쉽지 않다.
e.g. comple<u>tely</u>, absolu<u>tely</u>, defini<u>tely</u>, admitte<u>dly</u>, reporte<u>dly</u>, frequen<u>tly</u>

06. History Of Conflicts

0409history

1 마음으로 듣기

▸ This is [Today In History].
이 표현은 "이 시간은 '역사속의 오늘' 혹은 '오늘의 역사시간'입니다" 라는 프로그램을 소개하는 일반화된 방송용 어구이다.

▸ incarceration: 감금, 투옥

2 전치사 듣기

This is Today _____ History.

_____ April 9th, 1865, Confederate General Robert E. Lee, his Army of Northern Virginia trapped, outnumbered, and starving, met ______ Union General Ulysses S. Grant at Appomattox Court House, Virginia, _____ discuss terms _____ surrender.

Those terms were generous.

Rebels were allowed _____ return _____ their homes if they promise never again to take up arms ________ the United States.

Officers could retain their side-arms and all combatants could keep their horses and personal belongings.

The surrender effectively ended America's bloodiest conflict that has spanned 4 years and cost _______ 1 million casualties.

In 1917, holding a 2 _____ 1 advantage, British-led forces launched the Battle of Arras _____ Northern France ______ the 1st World War, gaining about 6 kilometers _____ German-held territory but ____ a horrific price of a quarter million casualties ______ both sides.

_______ this day in 1942, some 70,000 American and Filipino troops surrendered _______ advancing Japanese forces ____ the Bataan Peninsula, and assigning the captives two years ______ brutal incarceration.

Thousands died.

And on April 9th, 1959, the U.S. Space Agency NASA introduced 7 astronauts ______ the public.

Those seven would take part _____ America's first manned-space program, Project Mercury.

3 확장형

This is Today ______ ____________.

On April 9th, 1865, Confederate General Robert E. Lee, his Army of Northern Virginia trapped, outnumbered, and starving, met _____ _______ General Ulysses S. Grant at Appomattox Court House, Virginia, _______ ______________ terms ________ ________________.

Those terms were generous.

Rebels were allowed ______ ________ ______ _______ homes if they promise never again to take up arms __________ ______ United States.

Officers could retain their side-arms and all combatants could keep their horses and personal belongings.

The surrender effectively ended America's bloodiest conflict that has spanned 4 years and cost ________ ______ million casualties.

In 1917, holding a 2 _________ ________ advantage, British-led forces launched the Battle of Arras in Northern France _________ _______ 1st World War, gaining about 6 kilometers of German-held territory but at a horrific price of a quarter million casualties _______ __________ sides.

_____ _____ day in 1942, some 70,000 American and Filipino troops surrendered ______ __________ Japanese forces in the Bataan Peninsula, and assigning the captives two years _____ _________ incarceration.

Thousands died.

And on April 9th, 1959, the U.S. Space Agency NASA introduced 7 astronauts _____ _____ public.

Those seven would _______ _______ ____ America's first manned-space program, Project Mercury.

4 연결음 듣기

This is Today In History.

On April 9th, 1865, Confederate General Robert E. Lee, _____ _______ of Northern Virginia trapped, outnumbered, and starving, met with Union General Ulysses S. Grant at Appomattox Court House, Virginia, _____ __________ terms of surrender.

Those terms were generous.

Rebels were allowed _____ __________ to their homes if they promise never again to ________ _____ arms against the United States.

Officers could retain their side-arms and all combatants ______ ______ their horses and personal belongings.

The surrender effectively ended America's bloodiest conflict ____________ ________ ________________ 4 years and cost over 1 million casualties.

In 1917, holding a 2 to _____ ______________, British-led forces ______________ ________ Battle of Arras in Northern France during the 1st World War, gaining about 6 kilometers of German-held territory but ________ ______ horrific price of a quarter million casualties on both sides.

On this day in 1942, some 70,000 American and Filipino troops surrendered ______ _______________ Japanese forces in the Bataan Peninsula, and assigning the captives two ________ ______ brutal incarceration.

Thousands died.

And on April 9th, 1959, the U.S. Space Agency NASA introduced 7 astronauts to the public.

Those seven would take ________ ______ America's first manned-space program, Project Mercury.

5 응용형

This is Today In History.

On April 9th, 1865, Confederate General Robert E. Lee, his Army of Northern Virginia trapped, ________________, and starving, met with Union General Ulysses S. Grant at Appomattox Court House, Virginia, to discuss __________ of surrender.

Those terms were generous.

Rebels were _______________ to return to their homes if they promise never again to take up arms against the United States.

Officers could retain their side-arms and all _____________ could keep their horses and personal belongings.

The surrender effectively __________ America's bloodiest conflict that has spanned 4 years and _________ over 1 million casualties.

In 1917, holding a 2 to 1 advantage, British-led forces launched the Battle of Arras in Northern France during the 1st World War, _____________ about 6 kilometers of German-held territory but at a ____________ price of a quarter million casualties on both sides.

On this day in 1942, some 70,000 American and Filipino troops surrendered to advancing Japanese forces in the Bataan Peninsula, and assigning the captives two years of brutal __________________.

Thousands died.

And on April 9th, 1959, the U.S. Space Agency NASA introduced 7 astronauts to the public.

Those seven would take part in America's first ________________ program, Project Mercury.

07.

0605law

A New California Law

1 마음으로 듣기

2 수식어(형용사/부사) 듣기

A ______ law has been ____________ approved by the State Assembly in California to stop police officers' selling information to the media, ________ about celebrities.

The measure was prompted by ______________ report about the arrest _________ _________ of the Hollywood star Mel Gibson.

Peter Bowes reports from Los Angeles.

"When Mel Gibson got into a trouble, a celebrity website managed to get hold of a ______________ police report about his arrest."

"It was published on the Internet within hours of the star being stopped for drunk driving."

"The document revealed details of the actor's ________ tirade against the arresting officer, during which he was quoted as saying, "Jews are responsible for all the wars in the world."

"He __________ apologized for the remark. The website said it did not pay for the information."

"The politicians in California say the site's actions violated the movie star's _______ rights."

3 확장형

A _______ _______ has been _____________ __________ by the State Assembly in California to stop police officers' selling information to the media, especially ___________ about celebrities.

The measure was prompted by __________ __________ about the ___________ _________ __________ of the Hollywood star Mel Gibson.

Peter Bowes reports from Los Angeles.

"When Mel Gibson got into a trouble, a celebrity website managed to get hold of a _________________ __________ report about his arrest."

"It was published on the Internet within hours of the star being stopped for drunk driving."

"The document revealed details of the actor's __________ ____________ against the arresting officer, during which he was quoted as saying, "Jews are responsible for all the wars in the world."

"He ________ _______________ for the remark. The website said it did not pay for the information."

"The politicians in California say the site's actions violated the movie star's _____________ __________."

4 연결음 듣기

A new law has been unanimously approved by the State Assembly in California to stop __________ ___________ ___________ information to the media, especially about celebrities.

The measure was prompted by leaked report about the arrest _________ _______ of the Hollywood star Mel Gibson.

Peter Bowes reports from Los Angeles.

"When Mel Gibson _______ ________ _____ trouble, a celebrity website managed to get hold of a confidential police report about _______ ___________."

"_____ _______ published on the Internet within hours of the star being stopped for drunk driving."

"The document _____________ __________ of the actor's angry tirade _________ ________ arresting officer, during which he was quoted as saying, "Jews are responsible for all the wars in the world.""

"He later apologized for the remark. The website said it did not pay for the information."

"The _______ _____ California say the site's actions violated the movie star's legal rights."

▸ 가장 잘 들리는 영어 단어는?

① 자신의 영어 이름이다.

자신이 가장 잘 알고 다른 단어와 구분되는 고유명사이기 때문이다. 반면에 처음 듣는 다른 사람의 이름이나 지명 등의 고유명사는 알아듣기가 어렵다.

② 고유명사는 어떤 한정사나 수식어가 붙지 않는다. 역설적으로 알아듣기 어려운 단어가 어떤 한정사나 수식어도 붙지 않았다면 고유명사로 해석할 수 있고, 그것이 고유명사의 의미의 전부이다.

③ 물론 자신이 잘 아는 단어는 더 잘 들린다. 그러나 문맥과 일치하는 의미인지를 확인 하는데는 더 차원 높은 복잡한 지식이 필요하다.

5 응용형

A new law has been unanimously approved by the State Assembly in California to stop police ________________ selling information to the media, especially about ____________________.

The measure was ____________ by leaked report about the arrest last year of the Hollywood star Mel Gibson.

Peter Bowes reports from Los Angeles.

"When Mel Gibson got into a trouble, a celebrity website __________ to get hold of a confidential police report about his arrest."

"It was published on the Internet within hours of the star being _________ for drunk driving."

"The document revealed details of the actor's angry tirade against the ___________ officer, during which he was ___________ as saying, "Jews are responsible for all the wars in the world."

"He later apologized for the ____________. The website said it did not pay for the information."

"The politicians in California say the site's actions __________ the movie star' legal rights."

...08. □ 0212sen

Sen. McCarthy From Wisconsin

1 마음으로 듣기

▸ This is [Today In History].

이 표현은 "이 시간은 '역사속의 오늘' 혹은 '오늘의 역사시간'입니다" 라는 프로그램을 소개하는 일반화된 어구이다.

▸ McCarthyism: 정치적인 목적을 위해서 공산주의를 극단적으로 이용하는 주의, 사상 또는 운동

▸ fine: 미세한, 가느다란

The line .... is a very fine one.

2 어휘동사 듣기

This is Today In History.

On February 9th, 1950, U.S. Senator Joseph McCarthy of Wisconsin ________ into national prominence, ____________ that he ______ a list of more than 200 known Communists ____________ in the State Department.

A subsequent 4-year hunt for American Communists _________ the lives of many innocent people.

McCarthy was __________ when he _________ to __________ documentation for his charges.

And legendary newsman Edward R. Murrow _________ the finial blow to McCarthy's exploitation of fear for political purposes.

"The line between investigating and persecuting is a very fine one and the junior Senator from Wisconsin has ___________ over it repeatedly."

"His primary achievement has _______ in __________ the public mind, as between the internal and external threats of Communism."

"We must not ______________ dissent with disloyalty."

Ultimately, the Senate _______________ Joseph McCarthy.

Three years later, in 1957, he was dead from alcoholism and cancer.

▸ 어휘동사란?

① 본동사라 부르기도 하지만 동일한 것은 아니다.

② 독립적인 어휘적 의미를 갖는다는 면에서 조동사와 구분된다.

③ 시제문의 어휘동사는 조동사와 함께 쓰이며, 모든 조동사 다음에 온다.

④ 비시제문의 경우는 to-부정사구문의 'to' 다음에 원형으로 나오기도 하고, -ing 형으로 나타기도 한다.

3 확장형

This is Today In History.

On February 9th, 1950, U.S. Senator Joseph McCarthy of Wisconsin ____________ _______ national prominence, ____________ _______ he had a list of more than 200 known Communists ____________ ______ the State Department.

A subsequent 4-year hunt for American Communists ________ _____ lives of many innocent people.

McCarthy was ________ ______ he failed to provide documentation for his charges.

And legendary newsman Edward R. Murrow ____________ ______ ________ blow to McCarthy's exploitation of fear for political purposes.

"The line between investigating and persecuting is a very fine one and the junior Senator from Wisconsin has _____________ _________ it repeatedly."

"His primary achievement has ______ _____ _________ the public mind, as between the internal and external threats of Communism."

"We must not ____________ ____________ with disloyalty."

Ultimately, the Senate censured Joseph McCarthy.

Three years later, in 1957, he was dead from alcoholism and cancer.

4 연결음 듣기

On February 9th, 1950, U.S. Senator Joseph McCarthy of Wisconsin burst into national prominence, claiming that he _______ ____ _________ ______ more than 200 known Communists working in the State Department.

A subsequent 4-year hunt for American Communists ruined the ___________ _____ many innocent people.

McCarthy was exposed when he _______ ____ provide documentation for his charges.

And legendary newsman Edward R. Murrow delivered the finial blow to McCarthy's exploitation ______ _________ for political purposes.

"The line between investigating and persecuting ______ _____ very fine one and the junior Senator from Wisconsin has stepped over it repeatedly."

"His primary achievement has been in confusing the public mind, as between the internal and external ___________ ______ Communism."

"We _________ _______ confuse dissent with disloyalty."

Ultimately, the Senate censured Joseph McCarthy.

Three years later, in 1957, he was dead from alcoholism and cancer.

▸ 일반적으로 한국인에게 어려운 발음은?
① 우리말에 없거나 구별이 어려운 자음: [θ, ð, f, v]
e.g. sink/think, dough/though, base/vase, pace/face, of/off
② 조음위치가 애매한 모음: [i, e, æ]
e.g. sit, set, sat
③ 순자음도 순모음도 아닌 음: [l, r, w, j]
e.g. lice/rice, long/wrong, word/world, year/ear

그러나 더욱 중요한 사실은 이 단어들도 문장 안에서 쓰이면 우리의 또다른 인식능력인 예측력에 의해서 올바른 단어를 찾아간다는 점이다.

5 응용형

On February 9th, 1950, U.S. Senator Joseph McCarthy of Wisconsin burst into national _______________, claiming that he had a list of more than 200 ___________ Communists working in the State Department.

A ______________ 4-year hunt for American Communists ruined the lives of many innocent people.

McCarthy was exposed when he failed to provide documentation for his charges.

And legendary newsman Edward R. Murrow delivered the finial _____ to McCarthy's exploitation of fear for political purposes.

"The line between investigating and _____________ is a very fine one and the junior Senator from Wisconsin has stepped over it ________________."

"His primary ____________ has been in confusing the public mind, _____ between the internal and external threats of Communism."

"We must not confuse dissent with _________________."

Ultimately, the Senate censured Joseph McCarthy.

Three years later, in 1957, he was dead from ________________ and cancer.

09.

🖫0522us

Immigration To The U.S.

1 마음으로 듣기

▸ There is no question (about, as to, of, that ~): ...에 대해서 의심의 여지가 없다

There is no question (that) America is a nation of immigrants.

(미국이 이민자의 국가라는 것은 의심의 여지가 없다.)

2 접속사(관계사 포함) 듣기

There is no question America is a nation of immigrants.

______ you heard this program a week ago, you heard U.S. officials marked the 400th anniversary of the founding of the Jamestown settlement along the Virginia Coast by a small band of Europeans, seeking a better way of life in the new world long ___________ the United States was a nation.

Since then, millions from all over the world have sought the same thing.

In fact, immigration has been the lifeblood of the nation _____ it grew and expanded westward to the Pacific Ocean.

There have been waves of immigration to the United States from Europe ________ Asia.

Until recently, there has been little effort to regulate the flow.

________ in the past 40 years, there has been growing concern about the need to regulate _______ many people enter the United States to stay, especially those with skills __________ are needed.

That concern is intensified with the flow of illegal aliens, those _________ cross the border in defiance of law, seeking a better life for themselves ________ their families.

The United States has wide __________ forest borders with Mexico and Canada, ______________ vast coastlines on the East, South, _________ Western border boundaries, covering thousands of kilometers.

Controlling _________ comes in remains a challenge.

3 확장형

There is no question America is a nation of immigrants.

_____ _______ heard this program a week ago, you heard U.S. officials marked the 400th anniversary of the founding of the Jamestown settlement along the Virginia Coast by a small band of Europeans, seeking a better way of life in the new world _________ ___________ the United States was a nation.

Since then, millions from all over the world have sought the same thing.

In fact, immigration has been the lifeblood of the nation _____ _____ grew and expanded westward to the Pacific Ocean.

There have been waves of immigration to the United States from ________ ______ ________.

Until recently, there has been little effort to regulate the flow.

________ _____ the past 40 years, there has been growing concern about the need to regulate ______ _______ people enter the United States to stay, especially those with skills _________ ______ needed.

That concern is intensified with the flow of illegal aliens, those ______ ________the border in defiance of law, seeking a better life for themselves _____ ______ families.

The United States has ________ ________ ___________ borders with Mexico and Canada, _______ _________ coastlines on the East, South, and Western border boundaries, covering thousands of kilometers.

Controlling _________ _________ in remains a challenge.

4 연결음 듣기

There is no question America is a nation of immigrants.

If you heard this program a week ago, you heard U.S. officials ____________ _____ 400th anniversary of the founding of the Jamestown settlement along the Virginia Coast by a small _________ ______ Europeans, seeking a better way of life in the new world long before the United States _______ _____ nation.

Since then, millions from all over the world have sought the same thing.

In fact, immigration has been the lifeblood of the nation as it grew and expanded westward _____ _______ Pacific Ocean.

___________ ________ ________ waves of immigration to the United States from Europe and Asia.

Until recently, there has been little effort to regulate the flow.

But in the past 40 years, there has been growing __________________ ___________ _________ need to regulate how many people enter the United States to stay, especially those with skills _________ _______ needed.

That concern is intensified with the ________ _____ illegal aliens, those who cross the border in defiance of law, seeking a better _______ _____ themselves and their families.

The United States has wide and _________ ___________ with Mexico and Canada, and vast coastlines on the East, South, and Western border boundaries, covering ____________________ _____ kilometers.

Controlling who ___________ _____ remains a challenge.

5 응용형

There is no question America is a nation of ________________.

If you heard this program a week ago, you heard U.S. officials marked the 400th anniversary of the __________ of the Jamestown settlement _______ the Virginia Coast by a small band of Europeans, __________ a better way of life in the new world long before the United States was a nation.

Since then, millions from all over the world have ___________ the same thing.

In fact, immigration has been the lifeblood of the nation as it grew and expanded ________________ to the Pacific Ocean.

There have been waves of immigration to the United States from Europe and Asia.

Until recently, there has been __________ effort to regulate the flow.

But in the past 40 years, there has been growing concern about the need to regulate how many people __________ the United States to stay, ________________ those with skills that are needed.

That concern is intensified with the flow of illegal _________, those who cross the border in _________ of law, seeking a better life for themselves and their families.

The United States has wide and forest borders _____ Mexico and Canada, and vast coastlines on the East, South, and Western ___________ boundaries, covering thousands of kilometers.

Controlling who comes in ____________ a challenge.

10.

0115shark

Many Parts Of A Shark Are Valuable

1 마음으로 듣기

2 동사(조동사/본동사) 듣기

People _________ sharks for sport, food, medicine, and their skin.

Experts _______ the international market for some kinds of shark ________ _________ because many parts of a shark ________ valuable.

Collectors _______ thousands of dollars for the jaws of a shark.

Shark liver oil _____ a popular source of Vitamin A.

The skin of a shark _______ _____ _________ like leather.

In Asia, people __________ a kind of soup made from shark fins.

Experts ______ a fisherman _______ ________ a lot of money for even one kilogram of shark fins.

Finning, as it is called, ____________ cutting the fins off a live shark.

Many times, the fish _____ then ____________ back into the water.

The goal _____ to save space on the boats.

Animal activists ________________ this as cruel.

▸ 조동사(auxiliary)는?

① 이름이 암시하는 바대로 본동사를 도와주는 보조동사(helping verb)이다.

② 한 시제절에 조동사가 없을 수도 있고, 최대 4개까지 나올 수 있다.

Tense (Modal) (Aspect(perfect/progressive)) (Passive) + V ...

③ 시제절에서 맨 앞에 나오는 조동사에 시제(tense)가 표시된다. 이 조동사를 운용자(operator)라 부른다.

3 확장형

People _________ __________ for sport, food, medicine, and their skin.

Experts _______ _______ international market for some kinds of shark has increased because many parts of a shark ________ ______________.

Collectors _______ ________________ of dollars for the jaws of a shark.

Shark liver oil _____ _____ popular source of Vitamin A.

The skin of a shark can be used like leather.

In Asia, people __________ _____ kind of soup made from shark fins.

Experts say a fisherman ______ _______ ____ ______ of money for even one kilogram of shark fins.

Finning, as it is called, ___________ ____________ the fins off a live shark.

Many times, the fish is then ____________ __________ into the water.

The goal _____ ______ save space on the boats.

Animal activists _______________ _________ as cruel.

4 연결음 듣기

People hunt sharks for sport, food, medicine, and their skin.

Experts say the international market for some _________ _____ shark has increased because many __________ _____ a shark are valuable.

Collectors pay thousands of dollars for the jaws ______ _____ shark.

Shark liver oil is a popular ______________ _____ Vitamin A.

The skin of a shark can be used like leather.

In Asia, people enjoy a __________ _____ soup made from shark fins.

Experts say a fisherman can earn a lot of money for even one kilogram of ___________ ________.

Finning, _____ _____ _____ called, means cutting the fins off a live shark.

Many times, the fish is then thrown back into the water.

The goal is to save space on the boats.

Animal activists denounce this as cruel.

▸ 가장 안 들리는 단어는?

① 자신이 모르는 단어일까?

경험적으로 보면, 모르는 단어보다 알지만 (정확하게는 나중에야 알았지만) 그 문맥, 혹은 문장에서 쓰인 그 단어(의미)로 확인(identification)할 수 없어서 안들리는 단어로 판명되는 단어는 놀랍게도 대부분이 일음절의 우리가 잘 알고 있는 단어이다.

② 우리가 잘 아는 단어는 수가 한정되어있고(폐쇄부류), 주로 문법적 기능을 하는 기능어(function word)에 속한다.

③ 기능어는 더 이상 외울 필요도 없으나 문장의 구조를 만들어가는 중요한 어휘이고, 알면서도 들리지 않으면 문장 전체의 내용을 해석할 수 없게 된다.

5 응용형

People hunt sharks for sport, food, ______________, and their skin.

Experts say the international _______ for some kinds of shark has increased because many parts of a shark are valuable.

Collectors pay thousands of dollars for the ________ of a shark.

Shark ________ oil is a popular source of Vitamin A.

The skin of a shark can be used like ____________.

In Asia, people enjoy a kind of ________ made from shark fins.

Experts say a fisherman can earn a lot of money for even one kilogram of shark __________.

______________, as it is called, means cutting the fins off a live shark.

Many times, the fish is __________ thrown back into the water.

The goal is to save ____________ on the boats.

Animal activists denounce this as ____________.

11.

0415gene

A Genetic Explanation For Obesity

1 마음으로 듣기

▸ tax: 부담을 주다

... smoking taxes the heart ...

2 -ing형 동사 듣기

Researchers say they've found a clear genetic explanation for why some people gain weight while others do not.

The gene called FTO increases a person's risk for obesity.

Researchers __________ nearly 39,000 people found more than 60 percent of them had it.

Subjects with two or more copies of the gene had about a 70 percent higher risk of ___________ obese than those without it.

You can be young, fit, and eat right, but if you smoke, that habit is ___________ a toll on your health.

Researchers say ___________ taxes the heart by ____________ its ability to relax between beats, _____________ in decreased ______________ capacity.

In a new study, ultrasounds on smokers who seemed healthy showed multiple abnormalities _______________ impairment of the heart's left ventricle.

An apple a day may keep asthma away if mom eats them while baby is still inside the womb.

A new study suggests women who eat apples while pregnant may protect their children from _______________ asthma and related symptoms.

Researchers say the specific association found with apples may have something to do with naturally _____________ compounds inside the fruit that have been shown to have beneficial effects on adult lung function.

3 확장형

Researchers say they've found a clear genetic explanation for why some people gain weight while others do not.

The gene called FTO increases a person's risk for obesity.

Researchers ___________ ___________ 39,000 people found more than 60 percent of them had it.

Subjects with two or more copies of the gene had about a 70 percent higher risk of ___________ ___________ than those without it.

You can be young, fit, and eat right, but if you smoke, that habit is ___________ ______ toll on your health.

Researchers say ___________ __________ the heart by impairing its ability to relax between beats, resulting in decreased _______________ _______________.

In a new study, ultrasounds on smokers who seemed healthy showed multiple abnormalities ______________ ________________ of the heart's left ventricle.

An apple a day may keep asthma away if mom eats them while baby is still inside the womb.

A new study suggests women who eat apples while pregnant may protect their children from __________________ ____________ and related symptoms.

Researchers say the specific association found with apples may have something to do with naturally ___________ _____________ inside the fruit that have been shown to have beneficial effects on adult lung function.

4 연결음 듣기

________ ____ they've found a clear genetic explanation for why some people gain weight while others do not.

The gene called FTO increases a person's risk for obesity.

Researchers studying nearly 39,000 people found more than 60 percent of them ____ ___.

Subjects with two or more ______ ___ the gene had about a 70 percent higher risk of being obese than those _____ ___.

You can be young, fit, and ___ ____, but if you smoke, that habit is taking a toll on your health.

Researchers say smoking taxes the heart by impairing ___ _____ to relax between beats, resulting in decreased pumping capacity.

In a new study, _____ ___ smokers who seemed healthy showed multiple abnormalities indicating impairment of the heart's left ventricle.

An apple a day may keep ______ ____ if mom eats them while _____ ___ _____ inside the womb.

A new study suggests women who eat apples while pregnant may protect their children from developing asthma ____ _____ symptoms.

Researchers say the specific association found ____ _____ may have something to do with naturally occurring compounds inside the fruit that have been shown to have beneficial ______ ___ _____ lung function.

5 응용형

Researchers say they've found a clear genetic explanation for why some people gain weight ____________ others do not.

The gene called FTO increases a person's risk for _______________.

Researchers studying nearly 39,000 people found more than 60 percent of them had it.

Subjects with two or more copies of the __________ had about a 70 percent higher risk of being obese than those without it.

You can be young, fit, and eat right, but if you smoke, that habit is taking a ____________ on your health.

Researchers say smoking taxes the _____________ by impairing its ability to relax between beats, resulting in ________________ pumping capacity.

In a new study, ultrasounds on smokers who ___________ healthy showed multiple abnormalities indicating impairment of the heart's left ventricle.

An apple a day may keep asthma away if mom eats them __________ baby is still inside the womb.

A new study suggests women who eat apples while pregnant may _______________ their children from developing asthma and related symptoms.

Researchers say the __________ association found with apples may have something to do with naturally occurring compounds inside the fruit that have been shown to have beneficial _______________ on adult lung function.

12.

🖫0103taiwan

In Taiwan And In South Africa

1 마음으로 듣기

▸ 기능어(function word)와 내용어(content word)는?

① 기능어는 주로 문법적 기능을 하는 어휘로서, 수도 제한되어 있는 폐쇄부류(closed-ended category)이다. (전치사, 접속사, 한정사, 대명사, 조동사 등)

② 내용어는 주로 어휘적 의미를 가지고 있으며, 수도 무제한으로 늘어날 수 있는 개방부류(open-ended category)이다.(명사, 동사, 형용사, 부사 등)

③ 기능어는 일음절 어휘가 많으며, 약화되거나 앞뒤 단어와 연결되어 발음의 변화를 가져오기 때문에 오히려 알아듣기가 어렵다는 것이 청취의 아이러니이다.

2 한정사 듣기

_________ Chinese Government has accused _______ Taiwanese President Chen Shui-bian of trying to ruin ________ growing ties between Taiwan and the Mainland.

In _______ New Year Message, President Chen said that Taiwan was part of _______ world, not of China and _______ people have the right to decide ________ own future.

_________ American TV personality Oprah Winfrey is later today opening a new school she has funded in South Africa to give _____ education to girls from poor families.

_________ school, in _______ small town of Henley-on-Klip near Johannesburg, cost 40 million dollars to build.

It will initially have places for just over 150 girls.

From Johannesburg, Peter Biles.

For Oprah Winfrey, this is _______ fulfillment of ______ dream that began 6 years ago.

While visiting __________ _________ former President Nelson Mandela in December 2000, she promised to build a school for girls.

She has personally contributed more than 40 million dollars towards _______ project.

Oprah Winfrey, __________ own background was disadvantaged, says she regards education as the door to freedom, and she hopes ________ girls will be among South Africa's future leaders.

3 확장형

_________ ____________ Government has accused the Taiwanese President Chen Shui-bian of trying to ruin _______ _________ ties between Taiwan and the Mainland.

In the New Year Message, President Chen said that Taiwan was part of __________ ______________, not of China and _______ ___________ have the right to decide ___________ _______ future.

The American TV personality Oprah Winfrey is later today opening a new school she has funded in South Africa to give _____ ____________ to girls from poor families.

The school, in ________ ________ town of Henley-on-Klip near Johannesburg, cost 40 million dollars to build.

It will initially have places for just over 150 girls.

From Johannesburg, Peter Biles.

For Oprah Winfrey, this is _______ _______________ of _______ _________ that began 6 years ago.

While visiting _________ ________ _________ President Nelson Mandela in December 2000, she promised to build a school for girls.

She has personally contributed more than 40 million dollars towards ____________ ______________.

Oprah Winfrey, _________ ______ background was disadvantaged, says she regards education as the door to freedom, and she hopes ______________ __________ will be among South Africa's future leaders.

4 연결음 듣기

The Chinese ___________ ______ accused the Taiwanese President Chen Shui-bian of trying to ruin the growing ties between Taiwan ___________ ___________ Mainland.

In the New Year Message, President Chen said that Taiwan was ___________ _____ the world, not of China ______ ______ people have the right to decide their own future.

The American TV personality Oprah Winfrey is later today _______________ _____ new school ___________ _________ funded in South Africa to give an education to girls from poor families.

The school, in the small town of Henley-on-Klip near Johannesburg, cost 40 million dollars to build.

It will initially have places for __________ _________ 150 girls.

From Johannesburg, Peter Biles.

For Oprah Winfrey, this is the __________________ ______ ________ dream that began 6 years ago.

While visiting South Africa's former President Nelson Mandela in December 2000, she promised to __________ _____ school for girls.

_________ ________ personally contributed more than 40 million dollars towards the project.

Oprah Winfrey, whose own background was disadvantaged, _____________ _______ regards education as the door to freedom, ________ ________ hopes these girls will be among South Africa's future leaders.

5 응용형

The Chinese Government has ____________ the Taiwanese President Chen Shui-bian of trying to ruin the growing ties between Taiwan and the Mainland.

In the New Year Message, President Chen said that Taiwan was part of the world, __________ of China and its people have the ___________ to decide their own future.

The American TV personality Oprah Winfrey is later today opening a new school she has ___________ in South Africa to ________ an education to girls from poor families.

The school, in the small town of Henley-on-Klip near Johannesburg, __________ 40 million dollars to build.

It will ______________ have places for just over 150 girls.

From Johannesburg, Peter Biles.

For Oprah Winfrey, this is the ________________ of her dream that began 6 years ago.

While visiting South Africa's former President Nelson Mandela in December 2000, she ________________ to build a school for girls.

She has personally ______________ more than 40 million dollars towards the project.

Oprah Winfrey, whose background was _______________, says she regards education as the door to freedom, and she hopes these girls will be ____________South Africa's future leaders.

13. Talks Between Two Koreas

0510talk

1 마음으로 듣기

▸ 형태소(morpheme)는?

① 단어를 만드는 의미의 최소단위(meaningful minimal unit)이다.

② 어휘적 의미를 가진 파생형태소(derivational morpheme)와 문법적 기능을 하는 굴절형태소(inflectional morpheme)로 나누어진다.

③ 파생형태소는 접두사(prefix)와 접미사(suffix)로 나누어지고 중복해서 부착될 수 있으나, 굴절형태소는 접미사인 어미로만 쓰고 중복될 수 없다.

④ 형태소의 첨가에 의해서 발음이나 억양의 변화를 가져오는 경우가 있다.

2 주어 명사구의 명사 듣기

The first top-level military __________ between North and South Korea in the year got off for a rocky start Tuesday.

The _____________ was intended to focus on security for the test run of a rail line linking the two Koreas, but Claudia Blume reports the __________ insisted on also discussing the disputed sea border.

______________ of the two Koreas who started a three-day meeting at the Truce Border Village of Panmunjom on Tuesday said they want the talks to succeed.

After that ______________ of unity, however, came disagreement.

The main ______ of the talks was supposed to be the reopening of a cross-border rail line, which has been closed for half a century.

The two ____________ have agreed to conduct a trial run on May 17th, but the ______________ first wants the North to guarantee the safe passage of the trains, which cut across the heavily fortified Demilitarized Zone(DMZ).

If the Southern __________ thought the meeting's ________ had been set, however, they were wrong.

North Korea insisted on also talking about the two countries' disputed sea border.

Pyongyang does not recognize the so-called Northern Limit Line(NLL) in the Yellow Sea, the sea ________ drawn up by the United Nations at the end of the Korean War in 1953.

The North Koreans raised the same issue during military talks in May of last year, and those ___________ broke down when Seoul refused to discuss the issue.

Test runs on the reconnected rail lines were originally scheduled for last May, but Pyongyang called them off at the last minute without giving a reason.

Claudia Blume for VOA News, Hong Kong.

3 확장형

The first top-level __________ ______ between North and South Korea in the year got off for a rocky start Tuesday.

______ __________ was intended to focus on security for the test run of a rail line linking the two Koreas, but Claudia Blume reports ________ __________ insisted on also discussing the disputed sea border.

__________ _____ the two Koreas who started a three-day meeting at the Truce Border Village of Panmunjom on Tuesday said they want the talks to succeed.

After _______ _________ of unity, however, came disagreement.

The _______ _______ of the talks was supposed to be the reopening of a cross-border rail line, which has been closed for half a century.

The ______ ________ have agreed to conduct a trial run on May 17th, but ________ _________ first wants the North to guarantee the safe passage of the trains, which cut across the heavily fortified Demilitarized Zone(DMZ).

If the ________ ________ thought the ________ _______ had been set, however, they were wrong.

North Korea insisted on also talking about the two countries' disputed sea border.

Pyongyang does not recognize the so-called Northern Limit Line(NLL) in the Yellow Sea, the _______ __________ drawn up by the United Nations at the end of the Korean War in 1953.

The North Koreans raised the same issue during military talks in May of last year, and ________ _______ broke down when Seoul refused to discuss the issue.

Test runs on the reconnected rail lines were originally scheduled for last May, but Pyongyang called them off at the last minute without giving a reason.

Claudia Blume for VOA News, Hong Kong.

4 연결음 듣기

The first top-level military talks between North and South Korea in the year _______ _______ for a rocky start Tuesday.

The meeting was intended to focus on security for the ________ _______ _____ a rail line linking the two Koreas, but Claudia Blume reports the North ___________ ______ also discussing the disputed sea border.

Generals of the two Koreas who ____________ _____ three-day meeting at the Truce Border Village of Panmunjom on Tuesday said they _______ ______ talks to succeed.

After that display of unity, however, came disagreement.

The main focus of the talks _______ ________________ to be the reopening of a cross-border rail line, which has been closed for _________ _____ century.

The two Koreas have agreed to ______________ _____ trial run on May 17th, but the South first wants the North to guarantee the safe ____________ _____ the trains, which ________ ____________ the heavily fortified Demilitarized Zone(DMZ).

If the Southern Delegates thought the meeting's agenda had been set, however, they were wrong.

North Korea insisted on also talking about the two countries' disputed sea border.

Pyongyang does not recognize the so-called Northern Limit Line(NLL) in the Yellow Sea, the sea boundary ___________ _______ by the United Nations at the end of the Korean War in 1953.

The North Koreans raised the __________ __________ during military talks in May of _____ ________, and those talks broke down when Seoul refused to discuss the issue.

_________ ________ _____ the reconnected rail lines were originally scheduled for last May, but Pyongyang __________ _________ ______ at the last minute without giving a reason.

Claudia Blume for VOA News, Hong Kong.

5 응용형

The first top-level military talks between North and South Korea in the year got off for a rocky start Tuesday.

The meeting was ____________ to focus on security for the test run of a rail line ____________ the two Koreas, but Claudia Blume reports the North insisted on also discussing the disputed sea border.

Generals of the two Koreas who started a three-day meeting at the Truce Border ____________ of Panmunjom on Tuesday said they want the talks to succeed.

After that display of unity, however, came __________________.

The main focus of the talks was supposed to be the reopening of a cross-border rail line, __________ has been closed for half a century.

The two Koreas have agreed to conduct a trial run on May 17th, but the South first wants the North to ____________ the safe passage of the trains, which cut across the heavily ______________ Demilitarized Zone(DMZ).

If the Southern Delegates thought the meeting's agenda had been ______, however, they were wrong.

North Korea insisted on also talking about the two countries' disputed sea border.

Pyongyang does not _____________ the so-called Northern Limit Line(NLL) in the Yellow Sea, the sea boundary drawn up by the United Nations at the end of the Korean War in 1953.

The North Koreans raised the same issue __________ military talks in May of last year, and those talks broke down _________ Seoul refused to discuss the issue.

Test runs on the __________________ rail lines were originally scheduled for last May, but Pyongyang called them off at the last minute __________ giving a reason.

Claudia Blume for VOA News, Hong Kong.

14. The Battle Against Global Warming

0216warming

1 마음으로 듣기

▸ in his [State of Union] speech: 그의 (연방국) 연두교서에서

▸ 영어의 가장 힘이 센 (빈도수가 높은) 발음은?

① 굴절형태소 '-s[s/z]'이다.

② 명사의 복수형의 발음으로 쓰인다. (dog<u>s</u>, desk<u>s</u>, boy<u>s</u>, …)

③ 명사의 소유격의 발음으로 쓰인다. (father'<u>s</u>, today'<u>s</u> …)

④ 시제동사의 현재시제표지로 쓰인다.

e.g. Tom go<u>es</u> to school today.

⑤ 연속되는 자음의 맨 앞에 오는 발음이다.

e.g. <u>str</u>eet, <u>spr</u>ite, <u>scr</u>ew, <u>sl</u>ow, <u>sn</u>ow, <u>sm</u>ash

2 전치사 듣기

Government and business leaders _____ 20 of the world's largest energy-consuming countries will meet here ______ Washington this week to discuss ways to combat global warming.

VOA's Rosanne Skirble reports the object _____ the meeting is to help world leaders devise more effective ways to deal _________ climate change.

"David Miliband, British Secretary of State ________ Environment, Food, and Rural Affairs and a member of Tony Blair's Cabinet, comes to the Washington Legislators Forum _________ a simple message, "which is that the battle ___________ global warming needs the United States to be fully engaged and (that) the United States has a lot to gain __________ being involved ________ that drive."

"Critics say the United States took a step backward when it chose to reject the Kyoto Protocol, the global treaty _________ climate change."

"But the U.S. has argued that Kyoto was flawed and that mandatory curbs ________ the industrial emissions blamed _________ global warming would hurt the U.S. economy."

"While President Bush recognized climate change _______ a 'serious problem' in his State of the Union speech in January, he still opposes capping carbon emissions."

"U.K. Environment Minister David Miliband calls _______ a world commitment to reduce emissions especially _______ rapidly accelerating economies in developing countries."

"The Washington Meeting is part of an on-going dialogue that has shadowed G-8 summit meetings ___________ 2005."

"Delegates at the Forum will issue a consensus statement _______ climate change that G-8 President German Chancellor Angela Merkel will take _______ the July summit."

3 확장형

Government and business leaders __________ _______ of the world's largest energy-consuming countries will meet here _____ ___________ this week to discuss ways to combat global warming.

VOA's Rosanne Skirble reports the object ______ ________ meeting is to help world leaders devise more effective ways to _________ ________ climate change.

"David Miliband, British Secretary of State ______ ______________, Food, and Rural Affairs and a member of Tony Blair's Cabinet, comes to the Washington Legislators Forum _____________ ________ simple message, "which is that the battle _____ _____________ warming needs the United States to be fully engaged and (that) the United States has a lot to gain _______ _________ involved in that drive."

"Critics say the United States took a step backward when it chose to reject the Kyoto Protocol, the global treaty ________ _______________ change."

"But the U.S. has argued that Kyoto was flawed and that mandatory curbs ________ ________ industrial emissions blamed ______ ___________ warming would hurt the U.S. economy."

"While President Bush recognized climate change _______ ____ 'serious problem' in his State of the Union speech in January, he still opposes capping carbon emissions."

"U.K. Environment Minister David Miliband calls ________ _____ world commitment to reduce emissions especially ______ _____________ accelerating economies in developing countries."

"The Washington Meeting is part of an on-going dialogue that has shadowed G-8 summit meetings __________ ___________."

"Delegates at the Forum will issue a consensus statement _________ ______________ change that G-8 President German Chancellor Angela Merkel will take ____________ ___________ July summit."

4 연결음 듣기

_______________ ________ business leaders from 20 of the world's largest energy-consuming countries will _________ _________ in Washington this week to discuss ways to combat global warming.

VOA's Rosanne Skirble reports the object to the meeting is to help world leaders devise more effective ways to deal with ___________ ____________.

"David Miliband, British Secretary of State for Environment, Food, and Rural Affairs ________ _____ member of Tony Blair's Cabinet, comes to the Washington Legislators Forum with a simple message, "_________ _____ that the battle against global warming needs the United States to be fully engaged and (that) the United States has a lot to gain from being involved in that drive."

"_____________ ______ the United States took a step backward when it chose to reject the Kyoto Protocol, the global treaty on climate change."

"But the U.S. has ___________ _________ Kyoto was flawed and that mandatory curbs on the industrial emissions blamed for global warming would hurt the U.S. economy."

"While President Bush recognized climate change as a 'serious problem'in _______ ___________ of the Union ___________ ______ January, he still opposes capping carbon emissions."

"U.K. Environment Minister David Miliband calls for a world ______________ _____ reduce emissions especially in rapidly accelerating economies in developing countries."

"The Washington Meeting is _________ _____ _____ on-going dialogue that has shadowed G-8 summit meetings since 2005."

"Delegates at the Forum _____ _______ a consensus statement on climate change that G-8 President German Chancellor Angela Merkel will _________ ______ July summit."

5 응용형

Government and business leaders from 20 of the world's largest energy-consuming countries will meet here in Washington this week to ___________ ways to combat global warming.

VOA's Rosanne Skirble reports the object to the meeting _____ to help world leaders ____________ more effective ways to deal with climate change.

"David Miliband, British Secretary of State for Environment, Food, and Rural Affairs and a member of Tony Blair's Cabinet, comes to the Washington Legislators Forum with a simple ___________, "which is that the battle against global warming needs the United States _______ be fully engaged and (that) the United States has a lot to gain from being ______________ in that drive."

"Critics say the United States took a step backward ________ it chose to reject the Kyoto Protocol, the global treaty on climate change."

"But the U.S. has argued that Kyoto was _________ and that mandatory curbs on the industrial emissions blamed for global warming __________ hurt the U.S. economy."

"While President Bush recognized climate change as a 'serious problem' in his State of the Union speech in January, he still ___________ capping carbon emissions."

"U.K. Environment Minister David Miliband calls for a _________ commitment to reduce emissions especially in rapidly ______________ economies in developing countries."

"The Washington Meeting is part of an on-going dialogue that has _____________ G-8 summit meetings since 2005."

"Delegates at the Forum will issue a ____________ statement on climate change that G-8 President German Chancellor Angela Merkel will take to the July summit."

15.

□ 0327luck

The Beginning Of Bad Luck

1 마음으로 듣기

▸ 영어의 가장 힘이 약한 발음은?

① 중립음(schwa) [ə]이다.

② [ə]는 강세가 없는 거의 모든 모음의 발음으로 나타난다.

e.g. about, admit, allow, boxes, twentieth 등

③ 약화된 발음의 대표형이지만 다른 발음과 이어지면 다시 살아난다.

2 인칭대명사 듣기

_______ was once considered one of the luckiest people in the world, but _______ seems bad luck has followed Powerball winner Jack Whittaker ever since the day _______ became a multi-millionaire.

Now ______ accused of negligence in the death of ______ grand-daughter's friend, Jesse Tribble.

In 2004, Tribble died of an overdose at Whittaker's home.

Court records show Tribble and Whittaker's granddaughter, Brandi Bragg, had consumed cocaine and prescription painkillers.

Months after that, Bragg also died.

Whittaker was not at home when Tribble died, but Tribble's father says Whittaker is responsible for __________ son's death due to lack of adult supervision.

"He hadn't been doing drugs. He had been going summer school everyday where __________ was working."

Whittaker has no comment about the case.

"I can't talk, ______ give _______ a full interview when I get through with this trial."

Whittaker won the largest single jackpot in the nation's history on Christmas day, 2002.

He pledged to give much of ________ to charity, and he has.

But _________ also been robbed repeatedly.

And in one well publicized incident, he was drugged at a strip club, and half-a-million dollars was taken from _________ vehicle.

_________ also been arrested, sued, and recently claimed thieves had cleaned out his bank accounts.

3 확장형

_______ ________ once considered one of the luckiest people in the world, but __________ __________ bad luck has followed Powerball winner Jack Whittaker ever since the day ________ ___________ a multi-millionaire.

Now _______ _____________ of negligence in the death of his grand-daughter's friend, Jesse Tribble.

In 2004, Tribble died of an overdose at Whittaker's home.

Court records show Tribble and Whittaker's granddaughter, Brandi Bragg, had consumed cocaine and prescription painkillers.

Months after that, Bragg also died.

Whittaker was not at home when Tribble died, but Tribble's father says Whittaker is responsible for _________ ___________ death due to lack of adult supervision.

"He hadn't been doing drugs. He had been going summer school everyday where _________ _________ working."

Whittaker has no comment about the case.

"I can't talk, ______ _________ _______ a full interview when I get through with this trial."

Whittaker won the largest single jackpot in the nation's history on Christmas day, 2002.

He pledged to give much of it to charity, and he has.

But _______ _________ been robbed repeatedly.

And in one well publicized incident, he was drugged at a strip club, and half-a-million dollars was taken from ________ _____________.

_________ _________ been arrested, sued, and recently claimed thieves had cleaned out his bank accounts.

4 연결음 듣기

He was once __________ _______ of the luckiest people in the world, but it seems bad ________ _______ followed Powerball winner Jack Whittaker ever since the day he became a multi-millionaire.

Now he's __________ ______ negligence in the death of his grand-daughter's friend, Jesse Tribble.

In 2004, Tribble _________ _______ ______ overdose at Whittaker's home.

Court records show Tribble and Whittaker's granddaughter, Brandi Bragg, had _______ consumed cocaine _______ ______________________ painkillers.

Months after that, Bragg also died.

Whittaker was not at home when Tribble died, but Tribble's father says Whittaker is responsible for his son's death due to _________ _____ __________ supervision.

"He hadn't been doing drugs. He had been going summer school everyday where he was working."

Whittaker has no comment __________ _______ case.

"I can't talk, I'll give you a full interview when I get through with this trial."

Whittaker won the largest single _______________ ______ the nation's history on Christmas day, 2002.

He pledged to give _________ _____ _____ to charity, and he has.

But he's also been robbed repeatedly.

_______ _____ _______ well publicized incident, he was drugged ______ ___ strip club, and half-a-million dollars was taken from his vehicle.

He's also been arrested, sued, and recently claimed thieves had cleaned out his __________ _______________.

5 응용형

He was once considered one of the luckiest people in the world, but it seems bad luck has ________________ Powerball winner Jack Whittaker ever since the day he became a multi-millionaire.

Now he's accused of ________________ in the death of his grand-daughter's friend, Jesse Tribble.

In 2004, Tribble died of an ________________ at Whittaker's home.

Court records show Tribble and Whittaker's granddaughter, Brandi Bragg, had consumed cocaine and prescription ______________________.

Months after that, Bragg also died.

Whittaker was not at home when Tribble died, but Tribble's father says Whittaker is responsible for his son's death due to lack of adult ______________________.

"He hadn't been doing drugs. He had been going summer school everyday where he was working."

Whittaker has no comment about the case.

"I can't talk, I'll give you a full interview when I get through with this trial."

Whittaker won the _____________ single jackpot in the nation's history on Christmas day, 2002.

He _______________ to give much of it to charity, and he has.

But he's also been robbed repeatedly.

And in one well publicized incident, he was _______________ at a strip club, and half-a-million dollars was taken from his vehicle.

He's also been arrested, sued, and recently claimed ______________ had cleaned out his bank accounts.

Part 3

●●● 실전편1 01.

□ 0201gandhi

This Is Today In History

This is Today In History.

Making headlines on this day in 1948, many across India and the world were ________ ______ ________ ______ the assassination of 78-year-old Mahatma Gandhi, ______ ______________ _________ _________.

The British-educated lawyer was _________ ________ while walking to an evening prayer meeting.

A young man stepped from the crowd of about 500 and _________ ____________ ______ ______ _________ ______ ___________.

Riots quickly swept Bombay when news of Mr. Gandhi's death was received.

The Associated Press reported that 15 persons were killed and _________ _________ _________ ____________ ______ ______ _______.

●●● 실전편1 **02.** 0202muslim

A Muslim Cleric Released In Israel

In Israel, a military judge has ordered the release of a ________________ __________ ____________ ______________ from the United States.

Fawaz Damra is the former Imam at Ohio's largest mosque.

He was arrested in 2004 ______ __________ _____ ________________ ________ to the Palestinian group Islamic Jihad.

He agreed to deportation last year rather than face new terror charges.

Israeli authorities _________________ _____________ ________ after his deportation to the West Bank earlier this month.

In ordering Damra's release, the Israeli military judge said __________ ________ ____________________ ____________ to hold him any longer.

▸ Imam: (회교국의) 종교적 원수의 칭호 (=Imaum)

●●● 실전편1 **03.** 0203beach

The Beach Open To Everyone

No __________ ____________. It's the law.

The law at this luxury beach resort in Peru __________________ ______________ ___________ ________ getting in the water with their employers.

800 employees _____ ______ _______ protested against that law at a beach, South of Lima.

At first they formed a human chain _____ _________ ___________ and then they ___________ ___________ into the Ocean.

According to human rights organizations, this beach resort, known as Asia, is a place where social and racial discrimination _______ __________________.

Beyond being prohibited from swimming in the Ocean, domestic employees have reported _________ ______________ ________ ________________ and from just being on the Beach.

Peruvian laws __________ ________ the beach is open to all citizens.

●●● 실전편1 **04.** 0127smoking

Smoking Bans Are Popular

For the first time in the nation's history, more than half of Americans live in a city or state ________ ________ ____________ in workplaces, restaurants, or bars.

The movement for ____________ _____ began in Berkley, Calif., 30 years ago.

Smoking bans have also become more popular globally, ________ _________ _____ _________ in countries including Ireland, Italy, and Spain.

And being overweight may _________ _____ ______ of dying from heart failure.

New research indicates that obese patients hospitalized with heart failure __________ _____ _______ _________ than their lean counterparts.

The report, which appears in the American Heart Journal, showed that the "obesity paradox" may also apply to patients with ________ ________ or "decompensated" heart failure.

●●● 실전편1 05. ☐ 0203vista

New Operating System Vista

Microsoft has introduced _______ ____ _______ ____ the next big thing in software.

Microsoft calls it ______ _____________ _____________ __________ ________.

Five million people signed up to test its new operating system called Vista, and in its _________ __________ in a Times Square theater, chairman Bill Gates promised it would integrate the functions of the computer _________ ___________________ _______ _____________ better than ever.

"Homes are expecting now ____ _________ ______________, to be able to get their photos up in their living room, to be able to organize things."

Despite the ______________________ _________ of the launch, CEO Steve Ballmer _____________ most users will wait till their next computer to get Vista.

Though, the company insists _______ _________ _____ _____ _________ will dazzle the customers.

●●● 실전편1 **06.** 0205pharma

Pharmaceutical Giant Novartis

Protests were held in Washington and New Delhi, India on Monday against the pharmaceutical giant Novartis.

The company is ______________ ______ ________________ ______ ______________ ________ regarding drug patents.

Demonstrators say that if Norvatis wins the lawsuit, it will ________________ ________ ______________ ______ manufacture low cost generic drugs that are distributed throughout the global South to treat AIDS and other diseases.

Monique Wanjala spoke in New Delhi.

"I have been living with HIV for the last."

"This is thirteen years now, and I have been on treatment on ARVs since 2004, and this is because __________ _____ _______ _______ _________, and we are saying that if Novartis go through with this case, what does it mean to us as people living with HIV? It means that _______ ___________ _______ _____ ___________."

In Washington, activists from the Global AIDS Alliance ________ ______ ___________ _____ ________ ___________ to the downtown office of Novartis.

●●● 실전편1 **07.** 0206global

Concern About Global Warming

A new report on global warming ________ _____ _______ ________ and is very likely caused by man.

A key report _____ ________ __________ Friday in Paris by hundreds of scientists.

Lights were dimmed on the Eiffel Tower _____ ________ ____________ _____ the environment.

The winter storm that's pushed across the Southeast is making travel difficult, _____________ ______ _______________ and closing schools in several states.

A mix of snow, rain, and sleet have made _____ __________ _______ and caused at least one traffic death in North Carolina.

Mary Cheney, the Vice President's daughter, is brushing off _________ __________ ______ ____________ to have a baby with her lesbian partner.

Speaking at a Glamour magazine forum, Cheney says ______________ ________ children raised by same-sex parents are _____ _____________ _______ others.

●●● 실전편1 **08.** 0207block

Republicans Block Iraq Debate

Senate Republicans have ________________ ______________ _________ to consider a non-binding resolution critical of President Bush's troop surge in Iraq.

Minority Leader Mitch McConnell says ________ ___________________ __________ _______ __________________, not just one.

"We're not trying to _________ _________ ____________."

"We are trying to structure it in a way that is fair to the _________________ _________ in the Republican conference."

Democrats say the will of the voters on election day _____ _________ ____________.

An astronaut who flew last July on a shuttle mission arrested in Florida, _____________ _______ attempted kidnapping and other counts.

Navy Captain Lisa Nowak _____________ ______________, Police say, to confront a woman she believes is _____ _________ ______ ______ _______________ of a space shuttle pilot.

●●● 실전편1 **09.** 0208hool

To Cope With Football Hooliganism

The Italian Interior Minister Giuliano Amato said that when football matches _________ ___________ ______ ___________ in Italy, they will have to be played behind closed doors ___________ _______ ________________ ________ required safety standards.

He said that currently only 9 of the country's stadiums were considered safe.

Police powers will also be extended to cope with hooligans.

Christian Frazer reports from Rome.

"They _____________ ____________ ______________, and now they are telling the government has set out its tough proposals ______ ___________ _________ football hooliganism."

"Police will be given powers to arrest without warrant ____________ ______________ _______ ____________ _______________ up to 48 hours after the crime."

"And bans for _________ __________ ____________ _____ ________________ at matches will now apply to under 18s as well."

"The Cabinet will meet again on Wednesday to _______ __________ _____________ ________ ____ __________ _______."

"They are promising they will be introduced immediately and ______ ______________ ___________ next season."

●●● 실전편1 10. The Fate Of The Hmong

0209hmong

Government officials in Thailand say they will _________ ______ ____________ of about 150 ethnic Hmong refugees after several Western countries ___________ ____ ____________ accepting them for resettlement.

The United Nations Refugee Agency ________ ________________ ___________ ___________ today about the fate of the group if they were returned to Laos.

The Thai Foreign Ministry spokesman says the Lao Hmong, many of whom are women and children, have been returned to an ________________ _______________ __________ in the Northeastern Thai town of Nong Khai.

_____________ ________ __________ _______ there earlier today when Thai officials began to try to move them into _________ _________ _____ neighboring Laos.

●●● 실전편1 **11.** 0220crisis

For The Environmental Crisis

A Dutch oil trading company has agreed to pay a nearly 200 million dollar _____________ _________ _____ ___________ ___________ that led to a major environmental crisis in the Ivory Coast.

At least eight people were killed _________ _____ ________ ___________ ________ hundreds of tons of toxic waste in the Ivory Coast city of Abidjan.

Another 100,000 people ___________ ____________ _______________.

The company, Trafigura, says the payment is _______ ____________________ _____ __________.

Environmental groups including Greenpeace are calling the settlement ___________.

A class action ___________ _____ _________ _____ thousands of victims has been filed in Britain.

▸ class action lawsuit: [법률] 집단소송 (소비자 문제, 공해, 교통사고 따위로 인한 피해자들의 손해배상을 요구하는)

●●● 실전편1 **12.** ______________ □ 🖫0210friendly

Friendly Fire Killed A British Soldier

British Lance Corporal Matty Hull was killed during a friendly fire incident outside Basra ____ ______ _________ _______ of the Iraq War.

Two U.S. A-10 Thunderbolts __________ ________ _____ __________ ________ on March 28, 2003.

"Ambassador, why didn't _____ __________ _______ _____ ______?"

On Tuesday, _____ ____________ _____ _________ did not respond to reporters' questions about a _______ _____ _________ _______ that caught the _________ _____ ________ of the 2 American pilots on tape.

But now U.S. military officials have agreed to release the cockpit recording, ______ ____ _____ __________ by a British tabloid.

The Sun released what it claims is _____ ______ _________ between the pilots.

Pilot one says, "I'm gonna be sick," and pilot two responds with an expletive.

Then pilot one says, "Did you hear?," to which the second pilot responds with another expletive.

Finally, the first pilot says, (QUOTE) "____ _____ ____ _______, _______."

According to *The Sun*'s transcript, the other pilot ________ __________.

The Associated Press cannot confirm the authenticity of the tape or how _________ ________ __________ _________________ ______ it.

An investigation by the U.S. Military did not ____________ ______ _____ _________ ______________, concluding that the firing was accidental.

- expletive: 무의미한 말, 알 수 없는 말, 허사
- (QUOTE): 기자가 인용부분이 바로 뒤에 오는 것을 표시하기 위하여 가끔씩 사용하는 어 구
- *The Sun* released what it claims [t] is the tape: *The Sun* 신문은 (자신들이) 그 (비디오) 테잎이라고 주장하는 것(what)을 발표[보도]하였다.

●●● 실전편1 **13.** 0214bird

Birds Began Dying

In the ________ ____ __________ __________ ________ ______ outside of London, birds began dying this week.

Tonight the farm is sealed off, Police ______________ ________ ______ ___ ____________ and no possibility the virus will spread.

"No birds have left the premises and no product has left the premises. And so the disease on that premises _____ _______ ___________."

____________ ______ ______ _________ the killer virus was H5N1.

That's the virus that spread from South Asia to Africa and Russia, and last year arrived in Europe.

In 4 years, more than 160 people _____ _________ _____ _____ have died, most of them in Asia.

Scientists fear _____ ________ __________ ______ something more easily transmitted to humans.

That hasn't happened.

For officials now, _____ _____ ___________ _____ to discover if other birds are sick and if there is a risk of further spreading.

●●● 실전편1 **14.** ☐ 0219snow

Heavy Snow In New York

It's beyond a winter wonderland, and now parts of New York are ________________ _____ _________ serious problems.

More than 100 inches of snow has officially fallen, and forecasters continue to _____________ ______ ___________ ____________.

Central New York buried.

Parts of the region completely covered, ______________ ________ ________ ________ ________ _____ ________.

And with ____________ ________ _________ ____ ________ expected, New York's Governor has declared a State disaster emergency.

Crews are working hard to at least keep the streets clear, but ________ __________ _____ __________ _______________, especially since it's hard to even get anywhere.

Part of the problem now?

____________ ____________ to put all the snow.

Some snow plow drivers have been given permission to ________ ___________ ___

________ ________ open water such as lakes and rivers.

That might cause a problem ________ ______ ________ __________ ______ ______ __________, possibly creating localized flooding.

New York could be facing problems _______ __________ _____ _______.

What's worse, temperatures are due to dip to 11 degrees with a wind chill factor dropping to minus five below.

For many residents, all they can do is try to ________ __________ _____ _____ ___________ and look to forecasters to predict warmer temperatures.

●●● 실전편1 15. Free Hug Campaign

🖫0118hug

Need a hug?

It's not always an easy thing to find in the heart of the cold-hearted city.

A group of students were handing them out for free on the streets of Seoul, South Korea, recently.

They ________ ____________ _____ the free hugs campaign started in Australia two years ago.

"친구가 안기자길래 같이 안겼는데... "

This young woman says her friend _______________ _____ _____ ___ __________.

She says she liked the one feeling and decided this is a good movement.

Hug givers carry ___ _________ ________________ _________ ____________.

Interested?

Just come on over and start squeezing.

The hugs may be free, but _______ _______ _______ the huggers don't get anything in return.

The idea behind the campaign?

To engage in _________ _______ _____ ___________.

*the one feeling: 하나가 되는 느낌

●●● 실전편2 **01.** 0101vitamin

Vitamin D

Vitamin D is found ______ ________ ______ __________, and a new study suggests ______ _______ ________ _________ multiple sclerosis.

Researchers found that certain people _________ _________ __________ _________ of vitamin D in their blood were 62 percent __________ __________ _________ develop M.S..

Doctors say more study is needed _____ __________ ______ ________, but hope the finding _________ _____ a better understanding of the disease.

●●● 실전편2 **02.** 0516France

France Has A New President

Nicolas Sarkozy has ________ ________________ ________________ as the new President of France.

Outgoing President Jacques Chirac presented his successor with _______ _________ _____ ___________ ___________ ___________ as artillery salutes echoed outside.

Mr. Sarkozy is to go to the *Arc de Triomphe* to rekindle the flame on __________ _________ _____ _______ _____________ ____________ before taking a brief trip to Berlin to meet German Chancellor Angela Merkel.

Mr. Sarkozy will return to France and ________________ _______ _____________ tomorrow or Friday.

Mr. Sarkozy beat Socialist candidate Segolene Royal in a runoff election on May 6.

Britain's outgoing Prime Minister Tony Blair arrives in Washington later today for _______ _____ _______ _________ _________ with President Bush.

Mr. Blair's meetings with Mr. Bush today and tomorrow ________ _______ ________ _________ as Britain's Head of State.

●●● 실전편2 **03.** 0622missing

A Missing Woman And A Baby

There may be a __________ ________ in the case of a pregnant Ohio mother who disappeared, or it could be just coincidence.

About 45 miles away from where 26-year old Jessie Davis ______________, a newborn baby was found in a basket on a doorstep.

Investigators say the infant girl was ________ ______ and the umbilical cord was still attached.

DNA samples are now being taken _____ _______ _____ there is any connection with the missing pregnant woman.

According to relatives, Jessie Davis was expecting a girl and _____ _____ ______was July 3.

When her mother arrived at the house and __________ __________ __________ last week, it was also determined her cell phone and a comforter had been taken.

Police have _____________ the father of Davis's unborn girl who also is the father of her 2-year-old son.

Police patrolman Bobby Cutts Jr. _____ _______________ ________ his wife.

Investigators say Cutts has been cooperative and that they have no suspects at this time.

●●● 실전편2 **04.** 0611bill

Embryonic Stem Cell Research

Embryonic Stem Cell Research?

President Bush ______________ _______ ____________, and you can't sell human embryos even for _____________ _____ ______________ __________ for diseases and disabilities.

But Congress __________ ____________ the President.

They sent him pretty much the same bill he vetoed last year, ____________ _____ ______ ________ it again.

It's a bill that would allow Federal funding to support embryonic stem cell research which scientists say ______ _____________ ____________ – the possibility to help diabetes, Parkinson's, cancer, even spinal cord injuries.

The measure had strong public support.

It passed _____ __________ _____________ in the House and Senate.

But ____ ________ __________ ____ the two-thirds needed ______ ____________ the veto, and the President says he will veto it again.

●●● 실전편2 05. 0109diet

Reading About Diet

A new study suggests reading about diet and weight loss could ___________ ___________________ ___________________ for young girls.

A University of Minnesota study found that teenage girls ________ _______________ ________ _______________ _____________ about dieting were more likely, 5 years down the road, to __________________ __________________ _________________ __________ __________________ such as vomiting than girls who never read such articles.

It apparently ___________ ________ ____ _________ whether the girls were overweight when they started reading about weight loss, or whether they considered ________ _____________ ____________________.

●●● 실전편2 **06.** 0409history

History Of Conflicts

This is Today In History.

On April 9th, 1865, Confederate General Robert E. Lee, his Army of Northern Virginia ________, ____________, _____ ________, met with Union General Ulysses S. Grant at Appomattox Court House, Virginia, to discuss terms of surrender.

Those terms were generous.

Rebels were ____________ ______ ____________ ______ ______ ________ if they promise never again to take up arms against the United States.

Officers could _______ ______ ___________ and all combatants could keep their horses and personal belongings.

The surrender ___________ ________ America's bloodiest conflict that has ________ ___ ________ _____ ______ over 1 million casualties.

In 1917, holding a 2 to 1 advantage, British-led forces launched the Battle of Arras in Northern France during the 1st World War, ____________ ____________ ___ __________ of German-held territory but at a horrific price of a quarter million casualties on both sides.

On this day in 1942, some 70,000 American and Filipino troops _______________ _____ advancing Japanese forces in the Bataan Peninsula, and assigning the captives two years of __________ _________________.

Thousands died.

And on April 9th, 1959, the U.S. Space Agency NASA introduced 7 astronauts to the public.

Those seven would take part in America's __________ ______________________ ____________, Project Mercury.

실전편2 **07.** 0605law

A New California Law

A new law has been unanimously approved by the State Assembly in California to ________ ________ ________ ________ information to the media, especially about celebrities.

The measure was ________ ________ ________ ________ about the arrest last year of the Hollywood star Mel Gibson.

Peter Bowes reports from Los Angeles.

"When Mel Gibson got into a trouble, a celebrity website ________ ________ ________ ________ ________ a confidential police report about his arrest."

"It was published on the Internet within hours of ________ ________ ________ ________ for drunk driving."

"The document revealed details of the actor's angry tirade against the arresting officer, during which he was quoted as saying, "________ ________ ________ ________ all the wars in the world."

He later apologized ________ ________ ________. The website said it did not pay for the information.

The politicians in California say the site's actions ________ ________ ________ ________ ________ ________."

●●● 실전편2 **08.** 0212sen

Sen. McCarthy From Wisconsin

This is Today In History.

On February 9th, 1950, U.S. Senator Joseph McCarthy of Wisconsin ______________ ________ ____________ ______________, claiming that he had a list of more than 200 known Communists working in the State Department.

A ________________ ___________ ____________ for American Communists _____________ ______ __________ of many innocent people.

McCarthy was exposed _________ _______ _____________ _______ __________ documentation for his charges.

And legendary newsman Edward R. Murrow ________________ _______ ________ ________ to McCarthy's exploitation of fear for political purposes.

"The line between investigating and persecuting is a _________ __________ ______ and the junior Senator from Wisconsin has ________________ __________ _____ ________________."

"His primary achievement has been in ___________ _____ __________ _______, as between the internal and external threats of Communism."

"We must not ___________ ___________ ________ _____________."

Ultimately, ______ ___________ _____________ Joseph McCarthy.

Three years later, in 1957, he was dead from alcoholism and cancer.

●●● 실전편2 **09.** 0522us

Immigration To The U.S.

There is no question America is _____ __________ _______ ___________________.

If you heard this program a week ago, you heard ____________ _________________ _____________ the 400th anniversary of the founding of the Jamestown settlement along the Virginia Coast by a small band of Europeans, seeking ______ __________ ________ ______ ________ in the new world long before the United States was a nation.

Since then, millions from all over the world have _____________ ________ ________ ___________.

In fact, immigration has been the lifeblood of the nation as _____ __________ ______ ____________ ______________ to the Pacific Ocean.

There have been waves of immigration to the United States from Europe and Asia.

Until recently, _________ ______ ________ ___________ ____________ to regulate the flow.

But in the past 40 years, there has been growing concern about the need to regulate how many people enter the United States to stay, especially _____________ _________ ____________ that are needed.

That concern is intensified with ________ ____________ ________ ___________ ___________, those who cross the border in defiance of law, seeking a better life for themselves and their families.

The United States has _______ ______ __________ ______________ with Mexico and Canada, and vast coastlines on the East, South and Western border boundaries, covering thousands of kilometers.

Controlling who comes in _____________ _____ _________________.

●●● 실전편2 **10.** 0115shark

Many Parts Of A Shark Are Valuable

People ________ ____________ ______ sport, food, medicine and their skin.

Experts say the ____________________ ____________ for some kinds of shark has increased because many parts of a shark are valuable.

Collectors pay thousands of dollars _______ _______ _________ of a shark.

Shark ________ _______ _____ ___ _____________ ___________ of Vitamin A.

The skin of a shark can be used like leather.

In Asia, people enjoy a kind of soup made from shark fins.

Experts say a fisherman ______ ________ ____ _______ ______ ___________ for even one kilogram of shark fins.

Finning, as it is called, means cutting the fins off a live shark.

Many times, the fish is then thrown back into the water.

The goal is to ________ ____________ _____ _______ __________.

Animal activists denounce this as cruel.

실전편2 **11.** ☐ 0415gene

A Genetic Explanation For Obesity

Researchers say they've found a clear genetic explanation for why some people gain weight __________ ____________ _____ _______.

The gene called FTO _________________ _____ ____________ _______ for obesity.

Researchers studying nearly 39,000 people found more than 60 percent of them had it.

Subjects with two or more copies of the gene had about a 70 percent higher risk of being obese _________ __________ __________ _____.

You can be young, fit and eat right, but if you smoke, __________ ____________ _____ ____________ ____ _________ on your health.

Researchers say ____________ _________ ______ _________ by impairing its ability to relax between beats, resulting in decreased pumping capacity.

In a new study, ultrasounds on smokers _______ __________ ___________ showed multiple abnormalities indicating impairment of the heart's left ventricle.

An apple a day may keep asthma away _____ _______ ________ _______ while baby is still inside the womb.
A new study suggests women who eat apples while pregnant may ______________ _________ ________________ _________ developing asthma and related symptoms.
Researchers say the specific association found with apples may have something to do with _______________ ________________ _________________ inside the fruit that have been shown to have beneficial effects on adult lung function.

●●● 실전편2 **12.** ____________________ 0103taiwan

In Taiwan And In South Africa

The Chinese Government has accused the Taiwanese President Chen Shui-bian of trying to ________ ______ ___________ ________ between Taiwan and the Mainland.

In the New Year Message, President Chen said that Taiwan was ___________ ______ _______ ____________, ______ _____ ___________ and his people have the right to decide their own future.

The American _____ ______________ Oprah Winfrey is later today opening a new school _____ ______ ___________ in South Africa to give an education to girls from poor families.

The school, in the small town of Henley-on-Klip near Johannesburg, cost 40 million dollars to build.

It will _______________ ________ __________ _______ just over 150 girls.

From Johannesburg, Peter Biles.

For Oprah Winfrey, this is the _________________ _____ ______ __________ that began 6 years ago.

While visiting South Africa's former President Nelson Mandela in December 2000, she promised to build a school for girls.

She has ____________ _____________ more than 40 million dollars towards the project.

Oprah Winfrey, ________ _______ _______________ _______ __________________,
says she regards education as the door to freedom, and she hopes _____________
__________ _________ _______ ___________ South Africa's future leaders.

●●● 실전편2 **13.** 0510talk

Talks Between Two Koreas

The first top-level military talks between North and South Korea in the year got off for a rocky start Tuesday.

The meeting was ____________ ____ _________ ____ security for the test run of a rail line linking the two Koreas, but Claudia Blume reports the North insisted on also discussing the disputed sea border.

Generals of the two Koreas who started a three-day meeting at the ____________ ___________ ___________ of Panmunjom on Tuesday said they want the talks to succeed.

After that display of unity, however, ________ _________________.

The main focus of the talks was supposed to be the reopening of a cross-border rail line, which has been closed for half a century.

The two Koreas have agreed to conduct a trial run on May 17th, but the South first wants the North to guarantee the safe passage of the trains, which cut across the _______________ ______________ Demilitarized Zone(DMZ).

If the Southern Delegates thought ______ ______________ ___________ had been set, however, they were wrong.

North Korea insisted on also talking about the two countries'disputed sea border.

Pyongyang ________ ______ ______________ the so-called Northern Limit Line(NLL) in the Yellow Sea, the sea boundary drawn up by the United Nations at the end of the Korean War in 1953.

The North Koreans raised the same issue during military talks in May of last year, and _________ _________ __________ ________ when Seoul refused to discuss the issue.

Test runs on the reconnected rail lines were originally scheduled for last May, but Pyongyang ___________ ________ ______ at the last minute without giving a reason.

Claudia Blume for VOA News, Hong Kong.

●●● 실전편2 **14.** 0216warming

The Battle Against Global Warming

Government and business leaders from 20 of the world's largest energy-consuming countries will meet here in Washington this week _______ _______ _______ _______ _______ global warming.

VOA's Rosanne Skirble reports _______ _______ _______ _______ _______ is to help world leaders _______ _______ _______ _______ to deal with climate change.

"David Miliband, British Secretary of State for Environment, Food, and Rural Affairs and a member of Tony Blair's Cabinet, comes to the Washington Legislators Forum _______ _______ _______ _______, "which is that the battle against global warming needs the United States to be fully engaged and (that) _______ _______ _______ _______ _______ _______ _______ _______ from being involved in that drive.""

"Critics say the United States _______ _______ _______ _______ when it chose to reject the Kyoto Protocol, the global treaty on climate change."

"But the U.S. has argued that Kyoto _______ _______ and that mandatory curbs on the industrial emissions blamed for global warming would _______ _______ _______ _______."

"While President Bush recognized climate change as a 'serious problem' in his State of the Union speech in January, he still ______________ ______________ ________ ______________."

"U.K. Environment Minister David Miliband calls for a __________ ______________ _____ ___________ ______________ especially in rapidly accelerating economies in developing countries."

"The Washington Meeting is part of an on-going dialogue _____________ ________ ______________ G-8 summit meetings since 2005."

"Delegates at the Forum will ______________ ________ ________________ ____________ on climate change that G-8 President German Chancellor Angela Merkel will take to the July summit."

●●● 실전편2 **15.** 0327luck

The Beginning Of Bad Luck

He was once considered one of the luckiest people in the world, but ______ ________ ________ ________ ________ ________________ Powerball winner Jack Whittaker ever since the day he became a multi-millionaire.

Now he's accused of ____________________ ______ ________ ____________ of his grand-daughter's friend, Jesse Tribble.

In 2004, Tribble _________ _____ _____ ________________ at Whittaker's home.

Court records show Tribble and Whittaker's granddaughter, Brandi Bragg, ___________ ________________ cocaine and prescription painkillers.

Months after that, Bragg also died.

Whittaker was not at home when Tribble died, but Tribble's father says Whittaker is responsible for his son's death ____________ __________ _____________ ________ ____________ ____________________.

"He hadn't been doing drugs. He had been going summer school everyday where he was working."

Whittaker has no comment about the case.

"I can't talk, I'll give you a full interview when I get through with this trial."

Whittaker ______ ______ ____________ ___________ ____________ in the nation's history on Christmas day, 2002.

He pledged to _______ _______ ____ ____ ____ ___________, and he has.

But he's also been robbed repeatedly.

And in one well publicized incident, ______ ________ ______________ ______ _______ ________ ________, and half-a-million dollars was taken from his vehicle.

He's also been arrested, sued, and recently claimed ______________ ________ ______________ ________ his bank accounts.

●●●✔ 실전완결편 **01.** ☐ 0417today

What The World Happened Today

This is Today In History.

On April 16th, 1917, the leader of Russia's Bolshevik Party Vladimir Lenin __________ ________ ________ to Petrograd, modern day St. Petersburg, to ________ _____ ___________ against the weak post-Tsarist provisional government.

Lenin's promises to modernize Russia and to end the suffering of the Russian people ________ _______ ________ _____ _______ ________of the Soviet Communist Era.

On this day in 1947, former presidential adviser Bernard Baruch used the term 'Cold War' to __________ ______ ___________ __________ the United States and Russia.

Instantly embraced by newspapers, the term was _____ ________ _______________ for the battle between the two ______________________ _________.

The Cold War ended with the collapse of the Soviet Union in 1991.

On this day in 1964, prison sentences of up to 30 years were _________________ _________ _____ 12 British men of the 15 involved in the Great Train Robbery.

Eight months earlier, the men had robbed a royal mail train of 2.3 million pounds, approximately 7 million dollars in cash.

On this day in 73 A.D., the Great Jewish Revolt came to an end when Roman troops successfully _________ ______ ____________ __________ by the Zealots at Masada.

When the Romans entered the mountain-top fortress, they found its more than 900 inhabitants _______ __________________ _______________ rather than face capture.

●●● ✓ 실전완결편 **02.** ☐ 0504green

Green Areas In Cities

Earth and Sky.

Scientists are now looking at the green areas in cities – parks and playing fields – ______ __________ ________________ to provide a new kind of service to humans.

Here's ecologist Pamela Matson of Stanford University.

"So, for example, these green areas can be places where water that is running off from the city ______ ____ ______________ _____ ______ ________ and recharge groundwater."

"That's a service that the city could be taking advantage of."

She said scientists are looking at ___________ _____ _____________ of what they call "ecosystem services."

Those are natural resources – clean water, air, food – things Nature provides that people need.

Matson told Earth and Sky that some people in cities __________ _____________, __________________ and other items in their yards, balconies or community gardens.

The U.N. Development Program ________________ that 800 million people farm in and near cities.

"The agricultural areas that are just outside of urban areas, and even inside of urban areas themselves not only produce food, but it also can be a place where cities can recycle waste waters, where they can ______________ ______________ ________ that come from the cities themselves."

And that would save a whole lot of money in terms of, you know, having to take care of that waste disposal or water disposal elsewhere."

Sometime during 2007 or 2008, more than half of Earth's population _________ _____ __________ ____ _________.

....

▸ things (which) Nature provides [t] that people need
(사람들이 필요로 하는 자연(의 신)이 베풀어주는 것들)

실전완결편 03. 0108israel

Israeli And Palestian Territories

In Israel and the occupied territories, Palestinian officials are ________ ____ ______ Egypt has transferred thousands of weapons to ______ _____ _____ Palestinian President Mahmoud Abbas with Israel's cooperation.

An Israeli official told the Haaretz newspaper the Israeli Military help ________ _____ ________ of more than 2,000 rifles and 2,000,000 bullets into Gaza.

The _______ __________ was reportedly negotiated during Abbas's meeting with Israeli Prime Minister Ehud Olmert earlier this week.

Israeli Public Radio is also reporting ___ ________ __________ ___ _________ ___ reach Abbas's Forces in the West Bank within the next few days.

Meanwhile, Israel's ___________ _____ ____ ______ ____ ____ __________ inside the West Bank has ________ ____ _________ from the Bush Administration.

On Wednesday, the State Department said the new settlement would violate existing agreements and _____ ______ _____ ____________.

Israeli officials say the settlement will house up to 100 families who lived in the Gaza

Strip until Israel withdrew settlements there last year.
Israel had ___________ ____ _______ new settlement activity under the U.S.-backed road map.

Meanwhile in Gaza, Hamas spokesperson Ghazi Hamad criticized Israel's recent _______________ _____ ____________ _____________ inside the Gaza Strip.

▸ naked delivery: 무상배달

●●● ✔ 실전완결편 **04.** ☐ 0112bear

Polar Bears Need To Be Protected

They are the world's largest bears. They are beloved worldwide.

"They were cool!"

And now the U.S. Government says polar bears _______ ______ ________________.

"I really can't imagine a world without polar bears."

Scientific research shows that if _______________ __________ __________________ ____________ ____________________ _______ ___________, the polar bear could be endangered in less than 5 decades.

The Bush Administration has identified over-hunting, and for the first time ever, global warming _______ _____ _______ _____________ ____________ the potential demise of the species.

"I think it's a really bold step.

It identifies that there is a problem: that these bears are going to disappear if ____________________ _____ _______ _________ about the climate."

The proposed listing of these bears as threatened under the Endangered Species Act "comes in response to a lawsuit filed by 3 environmental groups who claimed the Government was ________ ___________ _____________ ____________."

"The Federal Government now has to take action to protect the bear and _________ ________ ______ ________ _______ _____ _________ is by reducing global warming pollution."

The Government ______ _____ _______ _____ ________ its proposal, but for visitors to the Central Park Zoo in Manhattan...,

"It is very sad because of my grandchildren. I want them to be able to enjoy a world that has all the animals in it."

... the great white bears can't be protected soon enough.

●●● ✓ 실전완결편 **05.** □ 0104belly

Belly Size

A new study suggests belly size may be ____________ ______ _________ ______ ________ alone.

Researchers found that obese people have more of a certain bacteria in the gut.

Scientists don't know if the bacteria makes a person fat or if the fat attracts more bacteria.

Further studies ______ ______ ________ ______ to find out.

Doctors ______ _____ _________ _____ ______________ Alzheimer's (disease) earlier.

It's believed the disease is caused by plaque build-up in the brain, but current scanners can't pick up early signs of it.

So researchers at UCLA developed an injectable isotope __________ ____________ ________ ___________, so it can be seen on scans.

Years of research are still needed before the test can be used on a widespread basis.

When _____ ___________ _____ predicting life-threatening heart problems, a new study shows sophisticated screening tests are no better than simple ____________________ ________ _____________.

Researchers look at 10 biomarkers that try to evaluate the risk for heart disease, but found (that) conditions such as diabetes, high blood pressure and cholesterol ________________ _______ _________ __________________ of risk for heart attack, stroke and heart failure.

••• ✔ 실전완결편 06. 0513danger

Dangerous Additives

In the world's largest country ______ __________ _____ ______________,
the concern is not over elections, but something more basic – what we eat.

China has promised to clean up its food industry after exports of ______________ _________ ______________ led to the deaths of dogs and cats in North America.

As VOA's Luis Ramirez reports from Beijing, environmentalists in the country are calling for a ______ ____ ____________ ____________, and more thorough enforcement of food safety laws.

The Chinese Government announced a plan this week to clean up its food industry.

The announcement was made as U.S. Food and Drug Administration officials visited China to investigate how Chinese melamine – a harmful additive – __________ _______ _______ ________ pet food in North America, killing or sickening thousands of dogs and cats in the United States.

Stories about poisoning from food products are nothing new in China, where manufacturers sometimes try to save money by ________ _____ __________that are both cheap and toxic.

In their statement this week, Chinese officials said the cleanup campaign will include improved monitoring of fertilizer and pesticide use, something environmentalists have been calling on Beijing to do for years.

Officials this week publicized the detention of managers from two companies that sold the contaminated wheat gluten and rice protein ______________ ________ ________ ____________ of dogs and cats in North America.

Analysts say the international attention is ____________________ _________________ among Chinese officials at a time when China's food exports are rising.

Some in the United States are calling for a ______ _____ ____________ from China of the same type of wheat gluten and rice protein in which the melamine was mixed.

●●● ✔ 실전완결편 **07.** ☐ 0812hydrate

Keep Your Body Well Hydrated

When _______ _________ ________ _______, the body gets going.

"Extreme thirst, lots of sweating. You will feel like _________ ____________ ______ ____________."

Four hundred Americans a year _______ _________ heatstroke.
Here's how your body tries to keep cool: when it's hot out, the brain ______________ ______________ down the spinal cord telling arteries and veins to move blood closer to the skin, where it can be cooled by the air.

Heat can also be carried away by sweat produced by the body's more than 2 million sweat glands.

But once humidity tops 75 percent and outside temperatures push 90 degrees, the body's ____________ _________ ______ ______________ don't work so well.

Symptoms of overheating include nausea, dizziness, headaches, and cramps.
Danger signs are confusion and not sweating, which may mean you're so dehydrated (that) you're _______________ ________ ______ fluid.

"The people most at risk during a heat wave are the young, the old and those taking certain medications."

"Cold medicines, for example, can ____________ _______ the body's normal cooling mechanism."

The key?
Prevention.

"Make sure you are well hydrated, and as often as you can, remove yourself from the hot environment."

Bring your animals with you.
The main way for dogs to cool off is _______ ____________.

Give them and yourself plenty of water and fluids with electrolytes.
Remember, what goes out must come back in.

▸ **electrolyte:** 전해물질

●●●✔ 실전완결편 08. 🖫0615delay

An Unforgivable Delay

"Janey went to hell, and all of us who loved her, we went to hell with her."

Looking like the Marine Corps drill sergeant ____ _________ _______, Jerry Ensminger poured out to a House Committee his overwhelming grief and anger over the death of his young daughter from leukemia more than a decade ago.

"Every time they stuck a needle through her bone in her hip to pull out ____________ ____________, I held her."
"And she screamed in my ear, "Daddy, daddy... Don't let him hurt me!"

When Janey was conceived, Ensminger and his family were living at Camp Lejeune, North Carolina.
Drinking tap water, a new Federal health study says, was contaminated with toxins up to 40 times current safety standards.

Chemicals from a local dry cleaner ___________ ________ Lejeune's water for three decades.
During that time, 75,000 people lived there and some 20,000 children were born.

The contaminants found in the water at Lejeune have been linked ______ ____________ _________________ to "birth defects and childhood cancers."

The Marines discovered the contamination in 1982, but allowed the families to keep drinking the water for another 5 years before they shut down all the wells.

It took until the year 2000 to notify families who drank the water, a delay ____________ ____________ ____________.

"What they have filled me with is a terrible resolve to expose their misconduct, their arrogance and their incompetence."

Eight-hundred fifty former residents of Lejeune have ____________ ____________ totaling 4 billion dollars for personal injury of death.
But it will be another year before scientific studies determine ____________ ______ ________ ______ ______ __________ for what happened to Janey.

- ▸ drill sergeant: 훈련담당 하사관
- ▸ was conceived: 임신되었다
- ▸ leukemia: 백혈병

●●●✓ 실전완결편 **09.** 0213sex

Penalty For Sex Offenders

_____ _____ the death penalty, a handful of States including Texas are considering _____ _____ _____ _____ _____ that are eligible for the death penalty.

In Texas's case, the Lieutenant Governor David Dewhurst wants to _____ _____ _____ _____ _____ _____. The Lieutenant Governor joins us now to explain.

"Good afternoon!"

"Good afternoon, Cathy!"

"Well, _____ _____ _____ _____ _____ for people."
"Let's say Michael Devlin, the man who is accused of kidnapping and molesting Ben Ownby and Shawn Hornbeck, was convicted and he was in your State."
"_____ _____ _____ _____ for the death penalty?"

"No, Cathy."
"_____ _____ _____ _____ _____ _____ _____ one of the toughest forms of the justice law, if not the toughest."
"And that is, if you commit a violent sexual crime against _____ _____ _____ _____ _____ _____ _____, you are gonna go to prison for at least 25

years, and if you get out, you're gonna ____________ ________________ ____
___________________."

"If [God forbid] you do it a second time, then the Prosecutors __________ _____
__________ _____ _____________ ______ _________ ____________."

"So, your theory is that, the death penalty will have a deterrent effect [YES] on the sex offenders [YES]."

"Is there any ____________ ____ _________ ________ ____?"

"Well, we've talked to police officers."

"I mean, for you and myself to be able to _______________ _______ ________ _________ is just impossible."

"But I've talked to judges."

"I've talked to police officers."

"I've talked to doctors."

"And if someone is rational enough to be able to _________ ____ __________, I could receive the death penalty if I do this a second time', we are hoping this is a huge deterrent."

"Because we've got a problem in every State."

"We've got 46,000 registered sex offenders here in Texas, ___________ _________ _____ _________ have victimized children."

"We've got to do everything that we can and ________ ______ _____________,

"Don't mess with children."

"Don't hurt our children here in Texas."

- Scaling back the death penalty: 사형(제도)를 다시 (마음 속으로) 저울질하면서
- God forbid: 절대 그럴리는 없겠지만
- deterrent: 억제재

●●● ✔ 실전완결편 **10.** 0215vitamin

Vitamin D Effects On Cancer

Meta-analysis has become an important tool in medical research.

In meta-analysis, ________ ____________ ____________ ______________ . _________

___________ ________________.

Sometimes taken together, several research projects can reveal something dramatically beyond _________ ________ ______ _________ ________________ ________________.

Now, the Moore Cancer Center at the University of California has done a meta-study of the effects of vitamin D, suggesting this:

"Vitamin D prevents ___________ _________________________ __________ _________

____________ _______________________ _______ ____________ of the breast, colon and rectum."

Co-author of the meta-study, Dr. Cedric Garland. If the risk of breast cancer and colo-rectal cancer _______ _____ _______________ _____ _________ by high levels of 25 hydroxy-vitamin D as this new meta-study suggests, it will be fantastic.

"Probably 50 percent we estimate can be prevented ____________ _________________

_________________ of vitamin D. Once the cancer is established, it appears vitamin D reduces _______ _________ _____ _____________ _______ __________________."

You get vitamin D _________ _________________, ________ _________ and in vitamin D supplements. Dr. Garland.

"It appears now that we have enough studies that ______________ __________ ________ ________________ ______ _______: yes, this is the time for people to start taking a minimum of 1,000 international units of Vitamin D per day. Women might consider taking even a bit more, 2,000 international units of vitamin D_3 a day."

So men and women would need different doses?

"We're recommending at least 1,000 international units a day for men. But for women, 2,000 international units a day is needed to suppress breast and ovarian cancer by about 33 percent. 4,000 international units a day would ____________________ _______ _________________ by approximately 50 percent."

Interesting, isn't it?

●●●● ✓ 실전완결편 **11.** ⬚ 0218wealth

The World Wealth Is Unequally Shared

This is 'In The News'in VOA Special English.

More than half of the world's wealth ______________ _____ just 2 percent of adults. A new study also found that 50 percent of adults _______ just 1 percent of all the wealth.

The report is from the World Institute for Development Economics Research, part of the United Nations University in Helsinki, Finland. The Institute says the study of personal wealth was ______ ________ _____ ______ ________ to include all countries and all major parts of household wealth.

Researchers considered possessions, property - all _________________ __________ _________________ ____________. They also took debts into consideration. They used information from the year 2000. And here is some of what they found:

Adults ___________ at least 2,200 dollars were in the top half of world wealth.

The richest 10 percent were ____________ __________ at least 61,000 dollars.

And the richest one percent had wealth of at least 500,000 dollars. Thirty-seven million people were ______ _________ ________ _______ ___________. More than half lived in the United States or Japan.

North America has only 6 percent of all adults but 34 percent of all household wealth. Together, people in North America, Europe and high-income countries ______ ______ ______ ______ __________ hold almost 90 percent of world wealth.

The study found that wealth is ______ __________ ________ than income. Countries where people earn a lot generally have a bigger share of world wealth than of the value of world economic production. The ___________ _____ ____________ ______ for countries where income is lower.

The Director of the Institute, Anthony Shorrocks, __________ _____ ______ ______ _____ ________ _____ all these numbers. If the world had only 10 people, he says, one person would have 99 dollars. The other 9 people would ________ _____ ________ _____ ________.

●●● ✔ 실전완결편 12. ☐ 0526dog

Trying To Outsmart A Dog

Federal Agency have long used dogs to help ______ ______ ______ ______ ______, but dogs require training, and they get tired and they get hungry.

Unlike the system, they call the HOUND.

"The hound system can ______ ______ ______ ______ ______, 7 days a week."

"Move over, Rover!"

"Police dogs can tell you if they find something, but they ______ ______ ______ ______ ______ ______.

New technology can do both."

"It actually not only detects explosives or drugs, but it identifies the specific type that you've found."

Sandia National Labs Engineer David Hannum developed the ______ ______ called the 'Hound.'

It looks like a shoebox with a 6-inch snout that works like a vacuum cleaner.

"As the air passes through the filter, it ______ ______ ______ ______ the

large organic molecules which happen to be the explosives and the drugs."
"And those molecules stick to the filter."

The metal felt filter is transferred to something called an ion mobility spectrometer, which can identify different substances because their molecules move ________ ____________________ ______________.

The 'HOUND' can __________ ______________ found in a fingerprint and it can identify 10 explosives and 10 drugs.

South Texas narcotics officer Richard Kirkpatrick says it used to ___________________ ______________ _______ _________ __________ to do that.

"We can get a result in a matter of seconds."

But he says dogs can ___________ __________ ______ ____________ from farther away, and he still chooses them first for detective work.

"I still love the canines, and of course ___________________ ________________ _______ ______________ for a very, very, very long time, and I believe science has still got ways to go to try to outsmart a dog."

"Good girl, Lassie."

••• ✓ 실전완결편 **13.** 0310health

New Health Guidelines For Women

New health guidelines for women from the American Heart Association, increasing the ________ ________ ________ ________ and suggesting a lot more women should take a half-dose aspirin everyday ________ ________ ________ heart disease and stroke.

More from CBS news medical correspondent, Dr. Jonathan LaPook.

"It ________ ________ ________ ________ women were classified as being low, medium or high-risk."
"But ________ ________ ________ ________ ________ some low-risk women actually have significant heart disease."

"We don't want women to wait until they have major risk factors for heart disease before ________ ________ ________ ________ ________ ________ ________."

"Lead author Dr. Lori Mosca urges women of all ages to stop smoking, exercise, ________ ________ and control blood pressure and cholesterol levels."

"I have three daughters..."

"Also new in the guidelines – a recommendation that older women, 65 and over, discuss with their doctor ________ ________ ________, even if

they have never had a stroke or heart attack."
"She recommended that I take an aspirin, that I lose weight, that _____ _________ ___________ ___________."

"Arlene Freidenburg is one of Dr. Mosca's patients."

"Yeah."

"In addition to the new recommendations about aspirin for older women, the guidelines also suggest that younger women under 65 should __________________ _____________ ________________ to prevent stroke, all women should consult a doctor because aspirin _________ ___________ ________________ ___________ ____________ like bleeding and ulcers."
"Other important findings - the American Heart Association ________ ____________ __________________ folic acid, and says hormone therapy and anti-oxidant vitamins do not prevent heart disease or stroke."

실전완결편 **14.** 0221valen

St. Valentine's Day Massacre

A lot of American workers receive some very bad economic news today – Chrysler is cutting 13,000 jobs, most right here in the U.S. Here is Anthony Mason.

Chrysler workers were calling it 'the St. Valentine's Day Massacre'.

"Disaster, Disaster."

This Newark, Delaware plant is one of two facilities ____________ ______ ____ ______ ________. "It's gonna be very difficult for a lot of people. And I feel bad. I'm in that group, too."

Chrysler ______ ______ ______ ____ ________ ________ last year.
To survive, the company says ____ ________ ____ ______ 13,000 jobs.

"What's wrong with Chrysler?"

"Well, the Detroit disease has hit Chrysler just like it hit Ford and GM." Csaba Csere, editor of Car & Driver, says this is the Detroit disease. Sales of ____________ ________ ______ ______ are way down, gas prices way up. Together GM, Ford and Chrysler have now announced more than 100,000 job cuts.

"We are very much ________ ____ ______ ________."

Dieter Zetsche heads Daimler-Chrysler, the company formed when the maker of Mercedes bought the American auto-maker back in 1998.

"Dear Dr. Z."

In Chrysler commercials, "What have been the benefits of the merger between Daimler-Benz and Chrysler?"

"Get in."

Zetsche has ___________ ______ ____________________ _____________, but today, he would not rule out putting Chrysler up for sale.

"Our thinking does not exclude any options. And this means ________ ___________ _______ ______ _______ __________."

"If Chrysler were to be sold, what would that mean for Detroit?"

"Well, the question is who would buy Chrysler? And the other American car companies aren't gonna be buying Chrysler."

In doubt for Chrysler workers now – not just their jobs, but _________ ___________ _____ _________ _______________ .

Daimler-Benz paid 40 billion dollars for Chrysler. If they do sale, _______________ _______ _______ they get less than half of that back, Katie.

"And Anthony, if Ford and GM won't buy Chrysler, who might?"

"The most talked-about name, Renault, the French car maker that owns Nissan. But _______ __________ __________________ _________, maybe a Chinese company, looking _____ ________ ______ __________ in the U.S. and establish a brand name. But it's all speculation."

▸ two facilities (which) Chrysler says [ ] it will close [t]: 크라이슬러가 폐쇄하겠다고 말하는 두 시설

●●● ✔ 실전완결편 **15.** 0227nixon

Nixon And Mao 35 Years Ago

Now on this date 35 years ago, __________ ______ President Richard Nixon? He was in China! And that was revolutionary – a conservative Republican politician decided to __________________ _______ ___________, at the same time that the war in Vietnam against Communism was raging.

We turn to Margaret MacMillan, a historian based in Toronto, author of the new book, *Nixon and Mao*.

"Uh, Richard Nixon ________ ____________________ ______ ____________ _______ the founder of Communist China, Mao Tsetung?"

"Nixon liked to think so, but perhaps he didn't know the ___________ _______________ _______________ about Mao's career. But what Nixon liked to say was that both he and Mao were _________ _________ ____________ ____________________ who had made their ways to the heads of very great powers."

"Considering President Nixon's record as an anti-Communist, you know, the trip was so surprising, so amazing. And I'm looking for ________ __________________ _________ _________________. Maybe would be President Bush going to Iran even while the U.S. is fighting radical Islam."

"I think that is a very good parallel. And certainly a lot of people were stunned when it was announced that Nixon was gonna go to China, and even more stunned when they actually saw him then meeting all the top Communist leaders. But you know what Nixon was thinking of, and I think he was right, was what ________ ________ ________ ________ ________ ________ the United States. And he was the man to broker an opening to China because he was such a strong anti-Communist. He really couldn't be criticized at home for having ________ ________ ________ ________. I think it helped actually. There was a wonderful line in the Star Trek movie, and someone says, "Remember the old Vulcan proverb, 'Only Nixon can go to China'."

"Do you suppose that the two leaders could have imagined where the relationship would go? Now, billions of dollars of trade, and frankly, ________ ________ ________ ________ the Chinese political system inside China."

"I think neither of them could have imagined it. I think Mao, if he'd foreseen what's going to happen, won't probably be spending in his grave or in his mausoleum in the middle of Beijing because he wanted China to remain ________ ________ ________ ________. I think you know if he looked around his own capital Beijing today, and saw the new hotels, the American businesses opening up there, the incredible skyscrapers going up, he will be stunned. I don't think Nixon had any idea that this was possible, although he lived to see a lot of it happening."

"Margaret MacMillan, author of *Nixon and Mao: The Week That Changed The World*, that week in 1972."

"Margaret MacMillan, thanks very much!"

"Thank YOU!"

참고문헌

다락원 (1993). 영어히어링 특훈. 다락원.
다락원 (2002). 영어리스닝 집중훈련. 다락원.
민종식 · 송홍한 (1990). 영어발음과 청취력. 현대어문사.
심민수 · 장경기 (2008). 현대영어학의 이론과 실용. 울산대출판부.
유윤환 (2007). iBT TOEFL 영단어 CHOICE 4000. 행담출판.
이찬승 (1998). Listening KNOW-HOW. 능률영어사.
장경기 (2005). 현대생성문법탐구. 울산대출판부.
장경기 (2010). 현대생성문법과 영어와 국어의 부정법연구. 울산대출판부.
장혜영 역 (2007). Isao Hyashi 저. TOEFL iBT 빈출 영단어 1700. 행담출판.
차경환 · 신동일 (2001). 영어청취론. 한국문화사.

Bromley, Karen D'Angelo (1992). *Language Arts : exploring connections.* 2nd ed. Allyn and Bacon. U.S.A.
Doff Adrian (1999). *Teach English.* Cambridge.
Lindgren, Clay Henry (1969). *The Psychology of College Success.* John Wiley & Sons. New York.
Markwardt, H. Albert (1966). *Linguistics and the Teaching of English.* Indiana University Press.
Miller, A. George (1973). *Communication, Language, and Meaning.* Ed. Basic Books. New York.
Rutherford, E. William (1987). *Second Language Grammar: Learning and Teaching.* Longman. London and New York.